"Scott Douglas is a very fine writer, a very funny guy, and someone who thinks and cares deeply about things of faith. When you combine those attributes (and ignore his sometimes questionable taste in music—One Direction! Really?), you get #*OrganicJesus*. And that's a good thing. This is a special book, suitable for people coming to Christianity for the first time, as well as for folks who have been following The Way a long time . . . but need a little lift in their Christian walk. Anne Lamott calls laughter 'carbonated holiness.' You'll laugh, sure. But you'll get a little carbonated holiness, too."
—ROBERT F. DARDEN, former senior editor, *The Wittenburg Door*

"A refreshing look-study-overview-reflection for Christians who want to be authentic, grown-up, and faithful."
—VINITA HAMPTON WRIGHT, author and editor

"Scott Douglas is forging a new path into multimedia literature . . . [and] taps into the heartbeat of today's tech-savvy spiritual searcher.

"Douglas understands that coming to embrace an organic Jesus means getting some dirt on your hands. He takes seriously this generation's value for authenticity. He does not shy away from the tough questions. And he is willing to openly lament life's tragedies. Here is #*OrganicJesus*'s true triumph. In the questions and situations over which he invites the reader to wrestle, Douglas displays a rich faith that has taken root in his own life. Don't let the medium in which this book is wrapped trick you into expecting a novel gimmick. #*OrganicJesus* is fresh, and just might plant the seedling desire of a new, raw spiritual quest in you."
—CHASE ANDRE, writer, speaker, academic, ChaseAndre.com

#**Organic**Jesus

finding your way
to an unprocessed,
gmo-free christianity

SCOTT DOUGLAS

Kregel
Publications

For bonus content download the free app
www.OrganicJesus.com/app
or visit www.OrganicJesus.com

Connect here
Twitter: @Scott_Douglas
Instagram: @thescottdouglas
Pinterest: www.pinterest.com/scott_douglas
Facebook: www.facebook.com/authorscottdouglas
LinkedIn: www.linkedin.com/in/authorscottdouglas
everywhere else: www.OrganicJesus.com/sharing-is-caring

For
Mordecai Max
La Counte

Contents

Introduction

Organic Jesus

#FaithMisadventures

Organic Fruit   **Organic Toilet Paper**   **Organic Jesus**

I used to be easier. Before distractions. And questions. And doubts. Before I forgot which way was up and which way was down. It was easier then. And it can be easier again. But I'm getting ahead of myself. Let's go back.

Back before the wrong direction.

Back to when things were right.

There were thousands there that day.

It was a larger audience than any baseball game I had seen in the same venue. I was seven, and the fierce preacher in the middle of the stadium spoke boldly about the person I had grown up hearing about every night before bed.

The preacher was Billy Graham, and this was his 1985 crusade at Anaheim Stadium.

Throughout this book, you will see a "Share" logo beside different images, polls, and text. If you visit www.organicjesus.com/share-this, you will see an option to share any of these ideas on your favorite social network.

As his sermon wound down and he began talking about knowing Christ personally, my mom and a woman from church asked my brother and me if we'd like to go onto the field and accept Jesus Christ.

My brother answered with an energetic yes, and I also quickly agreed. He was my older brother, and I'd have followed him anywhere.

Hundreds, perhaps even thousands, joined us on the field where we prayed. I was too young then to realize the consequence of my decision. Too young to know that there would come temptation, confusion, and even doubt. All I knew was that this Jesus guy I had heard so much about could be known even better, and why wouldn't I want that?

Nearly twenty years later, in 2004, an aging Billy Graham was on the last legs of his public ministry. I heard he was speaking at the Rose Bowl in Pasadena, California, and I couldn't resist attending.

Just as before, the stadium was filled to capacity with thousands of seekers, doubters, and believers—all there to see this great preacher who had delivered his message to audiences around the world.

But times had changed, for both Graham and me. Graham was now in his eighties. Parkinson's disease had taken a noticeable toll, and his voice and stance were frail. But the energy was still there.

I was now in my twenties. I was still a believer, but I had been raised in a generation that questioned everything and trusted no one. The Christ that I had accepted nearly twenty years before wasn't so simple anymore.

My childhood—my entire life—had been spent in what some have called a hotbed of fundamental or evangelical Christianity:

Orange County, California.[1] Christianity in my youth wasn't just the right choice; it was the only choice. Anyone who believed in anything else was crazy, or at least wasn't thinking logically.

That Christianity worked in high school, but in college it got a little trickier.

I began to hear from professors who gave a reason to be skeptical of belief, and it was one that, in academia, seemed to be unanimously accepted.

The older I got and the longer I studied, the more I saw that the Christianity of my childhood had holes in it that I had previously not seen. I didn't doubt my faith, but as I entered my thirties I started to feel troubled by it. I felt like I was looking at a two-dimensional Jesus, and I needed to find the next layer in order to hold on to faith.

WikiBreak SHARE

NOTE TO READER: I get it—you need to be constantly distracted with interruptions, and facts really don't mean anything. To help you out and keep you in the book, this book will have the occasional "Wiki Break" to help satisfy your urge to leave temporarily.

Anaheim has always had a frequent history of turning failed music venues into churches. After the success of Disneyland's opening in 1955, businesses flocked to the resort area, looking to capitalize on the boost in tourism. Leo Freedman was one such entrepreneur; he saw an opportunity to create a theater where tourists could see concerts, plays, and various entertainers. So it was that Melodyland opened in 1963, a few hundred feet from Disney's entrance.

By the late 1960s, the likes of Bill Cosby, Grateful Dead, and James Brown had all graced the stage. But the talents weren't enough to

---

1. It was home of the Trinity Broadcasting Network and of the stunningly tacky Crystal Cathedral (which made an appearance in the new Star Trek franchise and has since been sold to the Roman Catholic Diocese of Orange).

support the venue, and in 1969 the site was put up for auction. The Reverend Ralph Wilkerson purchased the property and the name was changed to Melodyland Christian Center. For several dozen years it was used as everything from a church and a Christian music venue to a theology school. The church ultimately moved from the property, and in 2003 the site was demolished to make way for one of Anaheim's most disastrous projects in recent history: The Anaheim Gardenwalk.[2] Any trace of the old building is gone.[3]

In 1987, the Celebrity Theatre opened behind Anaheim's City Hall to equally big acts, from the Red Hot Chili Peppers to the Beach Boys. The year of its opening, George Harrison, Tom Petty, and Jeff Lynne all traveled down to the little 2,500-capacity theater to see Roy Orbison. Backstage, one of the greatest supergroups in music history was born: The Traveling Wilburys. Yet again, despite the big names, the theater was financially doomed and closed its doors in 1994. It was revived under new ownership in the late nineties only to close again a short time later. In 2013, the property was purchased by The Rock Church.

In the midst of my finding that third dimension, everyone was trying to be original on Twitter. So I created @The140Bible, my attempt to condense each chapter of the New Testament into 140 Twitter characters. It connected with several thousand people for a reason all too common with anything today: our attention spans are getting shorter. Pastors have to deliver sermons in short, punchy, formulaic doses. It's rare for me to hear anything a pastor says in a sermon without being tempted to turn to my phone to research something it reminded me of. I might start with something like Occam's razor.[4] I end up ten minutes later reading a Wiki page

---

2. An outdoor mall that is largely abandoned aside from a few restaurants and small stores.
3. Even the namesake street name, Freedman Way, has been changed to Disney Way.
4. A rule that states everything should be explained in the simplest way possible.

about the next feature film of Héctor Elizondo,[5] and I have no idea what the sermon was even about.

But getting back to the 140Bible: by the time I finished the project, I began to question how we could deeply understand God in the digital age.

When I was in high school, I won a children's Bible in a church bingo game. It was full of illustrations and told the stories of the Bible in short doses—the kind of Bible meant to capture the attention of a nine-year-old.

Despite being baptized and a churchgoing Christian all of my childhood, I had never read (or even opened) the numerous Bibles that had been given to me over the years. The Bible was a big, intimidating book. But this Bible had pictures—lots of pictures—and I decided to do something I had never before done with a Bible: read it.

Despite years of Sunday school teachings, I had never understood the Bible—perhaps because I was too busy coloring pictures instead of listening to the lessons. But this Bible opened doors for me and made me want to know more.

Soon after reading the children's Bible, I began reading "real" Bibles from cover to cover. When I finished one translation, I started another. On the side, I began reading any theology book I could get my hands on.

First Peter 3:15 says that we should always be prepared to give a reason for the hope that we have. For me, that meant I should find out every reason why people don't believe in Christianity, so I began working on my college degree in comparative religions. All of this started with a teenager reading a dumbed-down Bible meant for a little kid.

---

5. Don't let the name distract you and lead you to a Wiki quest of your own—he won an Emmy for his role in *Chicago Hope* but is perhaps best remembered for playing Joe in the *Princess Diaries* movies.

Both the children's Bible and the 140Bible had the same purpose: to simplify the Bible. And yet one had been the gateway to making me more spiritual and closer to God, and the other had made me feel more . . . distant. The Internet could put everything at our fingertips—except God.

As I unloaded groceries from the car on a recent trip to the store, my wife, Diana, grabbed one of the bags and pulled out the package of toilet paper I had picked up. She read the label and then said, irritated, "This toilet paper isn't organic."

"Do they make it organic?"

"You can get anything organic." She tossed the paper aside. "I hope you realize that this is infested with inks and dyes. Don't complain to me if you're feeling itchy down there."

I walked to the bush in front of our house and pulled off a bundle of leaves. I handed it to Diana and said, "Here's some organic toilet paper for you—I'll take my chances with the dyes."

I'm not sure when the organic kick began, but it used to be much simpler: certain fruits and veggies were to be avoided if they were not organic. Over the years, though, it has gotten more complicated. Clothing, furniture, and now, apparently, toilet paper need to be produced organically.

USELESS POLL

The idea of organic living is . . .

A. too expensive for me.
B. a nonnegotiable. I work at Whole Foods just so I can get organic produce as soon as it comes in.
C. an option when it's available and I can afford it.
D. not for me until they make organic Pepsi.

To be part of this poll, visit:
www.OrganicJesus.com/useless-polls

SHARE

Wiki Break

Despite the boom of organic everything in recent times, the organic movement actually began dozens of years ago. It was first popularized by English botanist Sir Albert Howard. While some farmers were using the advances of the industrial revolution to make their crops cheaper, Howard was in India studying traditional farming techniques. His classic work, *An Agricultural Testament*, published in 1940, remains a seminal work for anyone studying the principles of organic farming.

In 1939, Lady Eve Balfour and Alice Debenham, influenced by the earlier writings of Howard, began the Haughley Experiment. The women did a side-by-side comparison of organic and chemical-based farming. Their findings were published in the now out-of-print book, *The Living Soil*. Among other things, the experiment proved there could indeed be health benefits from organic farming.

To some people, even me at times, my wife's fixation on organic is extreme. The question about toilet paper, however, made me wonder about something more deeply profound than toilet paper usually suggests: Can we live our spiritual lives in an organic way?

Why do we buy organic? Because we want something at its purest. We are seeking something with earth-made ingredients that haven't been treated or created with chemicals.

A few years ago, someone asked me how to get a teen interested in the Bible, and I told the person to give the teen a children's Bible. The longer you go to church the easier it is to forget one of Jesus's greatest lessons: the kingdom of heaven belongs to children.[6] To really understand God, it's best to strip everything away, to get rid of all the distractions and see God as a child might.

The troubled feeling I had been experiencing came from not having been told the complete story about who Jesus is. I needed to search and uncover the Organic Jesus—to take away the Wiki journeys to pointlessness and all the things that had created a flavorful, chemically produced, spectacle-driven Jesus—to strip it all away and return to the Jesus I knew before I ever owned a computer or heard of the Internet. The Jesus I innocently accepted at age seven.

There are two Christianities. There's the one you hear about at

6. Matthew 19:14.

church and then go home and forget about. But there's also the one you hear about at church and then go home and decide to learn more about. That second Christianity can be wild and wacky—because it involves a superhero.

If you really want to know this epic superhero you've entrusted your life to, then it's time to go on a journey to discover his origin story.

Getting Social

It's hard to do anything without running to your favorite social network to tell the world what you just read, said, or ate. To help you, I will suggest social media responses at the end of each chapter.

Twitter: Pick out a favorite passage from this chapter and add #OrganicJesus. Other acceptable hashtags include #OrganicToiletPaper and #FaithMisadventures.

Pinterest: Go to your favorite online store of choice and find the most bizarre organic products. Pin them to your board with #OrganicJesus.

Instagram: Print out a Christian coloring sheet. Color it, then scan it and add it to your Instagram feed.

LinkedIn: Seriously? You want to respond socially on LinkedIn? Perhaps you are a little *too* social?

Facebook: Add your favorite passage from this chapter.

WhichBibleHero AreYou?

NOTE TO READER: This quiz will make more sense when you get to the end of the book and get instructions. For now, just circle or remember your answer—

or skip to the end and ruin everything. You can also take the quiz here: www .OrganicJesus.com/bible-hero-quiz.

When people see you at church, what are they most likely to think?

    A. "They should be on the praise team." (+1)

    B. "They're in the right place." (+3)

    C. "They'll stick to this church in all situations." (+5)

    D. "They should be an elder." (+7)

    E. "Are they talking to themselves or God?" (+9)

    F. "What are *they* doing here?" (+11)

PartOne

Not Yo Mama's Christianity

Chapter One

The Passion of the Jew

#WayBackFaith

SHARE

Sad Jesus   **Catholic Jesus**   **Hipster Jesus**

Wailing.

That's the sound I remember most from *The Passion of the Christ*. It came from two rows behind and was occasionally followed by a tearful, "They're killing Jesus."

There were other vocalizations besides. When the movie began, a woman a few rows back loudly exclaimed, "Subtitles? They'll start talking in English, right?" There were lots of gasps and a surprising number of *Praise Jesus*es. The guy next to me nudged me early in the movie and said, with his mouth full of popcorn, "This is really sad, no?"

But it's the wailing I remember most.

Like everyone else in the nation, I had heard a lot about Mel Gibson's graphically brutal love song to the Messiah. I had heard three separate sermons from two different pastors on why I had to see this movie. Every magazine, secular and Christian alike, said the same thing. One magazine in particular suggested that not seeing this movie would be un-Christian.

I love gory movies. If it has the word *Tarantino* in it, I'm in. But I always felt conflicted about movies that portrayed Christ. There's no artist in the world who can accurately portray him, so why try?

So I didn't go at first. Not until my grandma guilted me into it. She had already seen it something like fourteen times. The same way some women went repeatedly to see *Twilight* and *Titanic*,[1] my grandma went to see *The Passion*; if there was a person who hadn't seen it, she'd tug their arm and pull them into the next showing.

Ten minutes into the movie, all I could think about was the Krispy Kreme donut shop that had opened in the parking lot of the movie theater. I know people were moved to tears by the movie, but the message was lost on me. It wasn't a movie about Christ's pain—it was a movie about some guy getting beaten to death. I understood that the whole purpose of a passion play was to show this, but the movie just didn't work for me. It didn't work for my stomach either; where other people would wince at the lashing, my stomach would growl and, loudly and inappropriately, remind me how much I wanted that donut.

Still, I stuck with it. According to some articles I read, it was my Christian duty to support this movie. If nothing else, I knew it

---

1. In college, a professor asked if anyone had seen *Titanic* more than once, and a woman raised her hand and joyfully announced that she had seen the movie twenty-three times. It had been out one month, and she went nearly every day.

would have a happy ending, and the two hours of blood would be worth it. The ultimate message of love and redemption would be revealed.

A funny thing happened on the way to the ending: a shadowy figure left the tomb—one could only assume it was Jesus[2]—and the credits rolled.

Before I saw the movie, I heard pastor after pastor say this was a great evangelical movie. But when I saw the ending, I just didn't get it. I couldn't imagine that any person who didn't already understand what the death and resurrection of Christ meant would walk away from this movie and say, "Now I get it!" If I wasn't a Christian, I would have walked away and said, "That was messed up what they did to Jesus." And that's it.

I looked at my watch as I walked out of the theater, and I sighed sadly. On top of having seen one of the most pointless and depressing movies of my life, Krispy Kreme was closed.

As I thought about the Organic Jesus, *The Passion* is one of the first things that crossed my mind. Despite my expressed distaste for the movie, it opened up dialogue for a topic that was frequently overlooked: the historical Jesus.

Jesus was God. And Jesus was man.

To understand the human nature of Christ, it helps to strip away everything the Bible tells us about his divine nature and the wise things he said, and to just think about what history may tell us about him.

There are many things with regard to any religion that have to be taken by faith. Religion by its very principle is not always logical; in essence, faith is believing in something you cannot understand with rational thought. But while Christianity may have fundamental principles based solely on faith, it is also grounded in fundamental truths that are based on logic. One such truth is that Jesus Christ actually existed.

---

2. Or a slimmed-down and slightly more fit Mel Gibson.

WikiBreak

The Passion of the Christ is a variant of something that has been around for hundreds of years: the passion play. Passion plays, which are themselves a variant of Easter plays, depict the trial, suffering, and death of Jesus.

The plays were always crowd-pleasers. (Who, after all, doesn't absolutely love to see the guy they worship beaten?) They became so popular that the fifteenth-century equivalent of liberal Hollywood swooped in and tried to secularize them. It got to a point where the plays were more like an episode of *South Park*, complete with obscene jokes and swearing. This, of course, upset the church, so they began banning "secular" versions. By the sixteenth century, the old-school plays were back, but their sexiness was gone, and the crowds went with it. Passion plays disappeared almost entirely until the nineteenth century, when they were rediscovered and haven't gone away since.

Today the biggest passion play is in New Jerusalem. Not *that* New Jerusalem; think Brazil. The New Jerusalem theater in Brejo da Madre de Deus was built in 1968 with one purpose: to host passion performances. Considered the largest open-air theater in the world, it features nine stages, sixty main actors, five hundred extras, four hundred crew members, and eight hundred costume pieces.

If you can't afford the cost of venturing down to South America, I suggest you read the book. It's called the Bible, and it has a lot of scenes that didn't make it into the play.

Full disclosure: we're about to get historical. After this point, there are going to be a lot of references to historical events, seminars, and other things some people do not find interesting. Don't worry. It's going to be okay. I'll get you through it.

If you feel intimidated, music helps. Following is a playlist of seven songs about historical events to get you in the mood.

"1913 Massacre" by Woody Guthrie. It's never a good idea to yell "Fire!" in a crowded building when there is no fire. The event happened on December 24, 1913, at the Italian Hall in Calumet, Michigan. Seventy-three people were killed while fleeing the building.

"April 29, 1992 (Miami)" by Sublime. Depending on your view, this song is about the 1992 Los Angeles Riots. Though the name of the song gives the correct date of the riots, the lyrics refer to April 26. Apparently the band members were so moved by the event that they couldn't get the date right.

"The Lords of Salem" by Rob Zombie. Zombie goes old-school on this classic ditty about the Salem Witch Trials.

"When the Tigers Broke Free" by Pink Floyd. This song describes the death of Roger Waters's father in Operation Shingle, a WWII amphibious landing battle that took place several months before the Battle of Normandy in Italy.

"Back to December" by Taylor Swift. The song is allegedly about Swift's breakup with Taylor Lautner. Though the song doesn't mention it, one can speculate that Swift felt forced to break up with Lautner upon realizing that if they ever married, they'd have the exact same name.

"Suffer Little Children" by The Smiths. The song is about the notorious Moors Murders. The Moors Murders took place in England between 1963 and 1965. During those years, Ian Brady and Myra Hindley murdered five children between the ages of ten and seventeen.

"Louisiana 1927" by Randy Newman. He may be better known for film scores, but Newman is also a great storyteller. Such is the case with this song about the Great Mississippi Flood of 1927, which was the most destructive river flood in US history.

It all began on a dark and stormy night in the seventeenth century. It was England, so let's just say it was gloomy too. The printing press had been alive and kicking out books for quite some time, and people were starting to get . . . enlightened. (Maybe that's how they came up with the term for that period: the Age of Enlightenment?)

It's hard to place a firm starting date, but we can certainly point out some of the key players: Baruch Spinoza, Voltaire, and Isaac Newton. They were the original bad boys of intellectualism, and they were on a mission to change things up.

Amongst other contributions, these three said, "Just because we've always believed this way doesn't mean we have to continue to believe this way." It was a naughty way of thinking, and they took some heat for it.

At first people started to rethink things like science and math. It didn't take long for someone to get religious and bring Christ into the Enlightenment conversation. And so it was that scholars began to wonder if there was more to Jesus than what the Bible said. They began to look for historical evidence.

Albert Schweitzer is the one responsible for coining the term *historical Jesus* when he wrote the book *The Quest of the Historical Jesus* in 1906.[3] Schweitzer was not the first, however, to provide scholarly research into the historicity of Christ. The quest for the historical Jesus first caught on in the eighteenth century, most notably with David Strauss, who popularized what would be known as the "Myth Theory" when he published *Das Leben Jesu, Kritisch Bearbeitet* (translation: *The Life of Jesus, Critically Examined*).[4]

Over the past several hundred years, there have been several variants of the Christ myth theory. Each variant essentially says one of three things:

---

3. Yes, the very Albert Schweitzer who appeared (fictionalized) in not one but two episodes of *The Young Indiana Jones Chronicles*.
4. Another popular myth supporter was Bruno Bauer, a mentor of Karl Marx.

1. There was no historic figure named Jesus; Jesus was, in fact, invented by early Christians.
2. There was "technically" a person named Jesus, but all the teachings and miracles are either made up or metaphoric/symbolic.
3. Jesus is really a composite of several different people over a period of time.

The problem with all three of these theories is simple: there's historic evidence from nonbelievers that debunks them.

Which leads us to (*drumroll*) . . . The Quest for the Historical Jesus (*wild applause*).

My introduction to the so-called "historical Jesus" took place when I was a teen. The minister was preaching a rather windy sermon about who Christ was. At the end, he paused, looked dramatically at his notes, and then made a startling pronouncement: "Over my dozens of years of scholarly reading and research, I have come to the conclusion that Christ could not have performed the miracles in the Bible. He was an amazing teacher—perhaps greater than any we will ever know—and his teachings should be followed and abided."

What surprised me more than the minister's declaration was that he was not fired. Many people at the church concluded that it was all a giant misunderstanding and he didn't mean it "like that."

But he did mean it "like that," and he preached it again in several other sermons.

In the end, it didn't matter to most of the people in the church. They were there for the long haul, and a greater sin than saying you didn't believe in the miracles of Christ was saying you did not believe in the church. Church, for a lot of people, is the foundation of their life. The message is just a happy coincidence.

Not until a year after that sermon did I again encounter the historical Jesus. It was during an introduction to religion course that

I took during my first year in college. The course covered all the major religions, from Eastern religions like Hinduism to Western religions like Judaism.

Christianity was taught halfway through the class and was met with the most interest. The teacher, an energetic older man whose clothes got drenched in sweat halfway through his lectures, began his lecture with these words: "Everything you learned about Jesus from Sunday school . . . is a lie."

There were three quests for the historical Jesus,[5] each more controversial than the previous one. The third was the most controversial and the one most commonly referred to in colleges across the country. It was also the one my former minister so fondly followed. Among other things, it questioned the plausibility of Jesus's miraculous actions.

USELESS POLL

My favorite historical Bible movie is . . .

A. *The Ten Commandments.*
B. *King of Kings.*
C. *The Life of Brian.*
D. any VeggieTales movie.
E. *Noah.*

To be part of this poll, visit:
www.OrganicJesus.com/useless-polls

My college professor was eager to discuss one of the greatest groups in modern Christian scholarship: The Jesus Seminars. The Jesus Seminars was made popular in the 1980s and 1990s. It was made up of 150 scholars who would sit around and vote about what they believed Jesus did or didn't do by casting votes with colored beads. They essentially re-created the Gospels by removing anything they did not think was true.

As hard as I tried to listen to the professor explain his fondness for his beloved Jesus Seminars, it was hard to take him seriously when he referenced the beads. His description of old men tossing around beads felt more like Mardi Gras than academia.

"They said why they believed or didn't believe though, right?" a student asked at one point.

The professor looked at him, confused. "They didn't need to—

---

5. The first began in the nineteenth century, when literally hundreds of "biographies" of Jesus were published.

the action of throwing the beads said it all." He added, as a way of clearing up all confusion, "The beads were colored."

When I began my own quest to see who Jesus *really* was, I was almost immediately reintroduced to the now disbanded Jesus Seminars. Their quest for the historical Jesus may be a bit liberal for some, but it did do one important thing: it proved that Jesus did exist. Even the most liberal religious scholars will agree on two things: one, the baptism of Jesus happened; and two, the crucifixion was real.

There are two notable historic historians people talk about when they mention the history of Christ. The first is Titus Flavius Josephus (AD 37–ca. 100).[6] Josephus was a historian who wrote about different events of the Roman Empire. A Jewish soldier who fought in the First Jewish-Roman War as head of the Jewish forces in Galilee, Josephus after the war became a Roman citizen and friend to the emperor's son. His most important contribution to Christianity was his book *Antiquities of the Jews*. It's important for this reason: Josephus was a non-Christian who references Jesus Christ. The book provides three key passages that help prove the existence of Jesus.

In book 20, chapter 9, section 1, Josephus writes regarding the crucifixion: "He assembled the Sanhedrin of judges, and brought before them the brother of Jesus, who was called Christ, whose name was James, and some others."[7]

In 18.5.2, Josephus writes of John the Baptist, "Now some of the Jews thought that the destruction of Herod's army came from God, and that very justly, as a punishment of what he did against John, that was called the Baptist: for Herod slew him, who was a good man."

---

6. Sorry . . . more history stuff follows. You have the music on, right?

7. All passages from Josephus's work were translated by William Whiston.

Finally, in 18.3.3, Josephus writes,

> Now there was about this time Jesus, a wise man, if it be
> lawful to call him a man; for he was a doer of wonderful
> works, a teacher of such men as receive the truth with
> pleasure. He drew over to him both many of the Jews
> and many of the Gentiles. He was [the] Christ. And when
> Pilate, at the suggestion of the principal men amongst us,
> had condemned him to the cross, those that loved him
> at the first did not forsake him; for he appeared to them
> alive again the third day; as the divine prophets had fore-
> told these and ten thousand other wonderful things con-
> cerning him. And the tribe of Christians, so named from
> him, are not extinct at this day.

Some scholars have tried to discredit this third passage, saying
the content was added at a later date by someone else; this certainly
might be true, but the writing style does appear to match Josephus.
The fact is, however, there are two passages that are almost unanimously undisputed, and a third that, while debatable, certainly
seems likely.

The other historian of note was Gaius Suetonius Tranquillus
(or Suetonius, as he was known to his homeboys). Suetonius was a
Roman historian who is best known for writing biographies about
Roman rulers. In his work *Claudius*, Suetonius says, "Since the
Jews constantly made disturbances at the instigation of Chrestus,
he [the emperor] expelled them to Rome."[8] Nearly every scholar
agrees that Chrestus is a reference to Christ.[9]

Those are the two main writings commonly referenced; however,
a slew of other historians provide further corroboration. Publius (or
Gaius) Cornelius Tacitus, a Roman senator and historian, is one.

---

8. Translated by J. C. Rolfe.
9. The text is also believed to be paralleled in Acts 18:2.

His last work, *The Annals,* is the one most important to the history of the Christ. In *The Annals* 15.44, he writes,

> Consequently, to get rid of the report, Nero fastened the guilt and inflicted the most exquisite tortures on a class hated for their abominations, called Christians by the populace. Christus, from whom the name had its origin, suffered the extreme penalty during the reign of Tiberius at the hands of one of our procurators, Pontius Pilatus, and a most mischievous superstition, thus checked for the moment, again broke out not only in Judæa, the first source of the evil, but even in Rome, where all things hideous and shameful from every part of the world find their centre and become popular. Accordingly, an arrest was first made of all who pleaded guilty; then, upon their information, an immense multitude was convicted, not so much of the crime of firing the city, as of hatred against mankind.[10]

Mara Bar-Serapion is a bit of a mystery. It's known that he was a philosopher, and that's about it. He's most known for a letter he wrote to his son. The letter contains this passage: "What advantage did the Jews gain from executing their wise king? It was just after that their kingdom was abolished."[11]

The reference to a king of the Jews is of note.

There were other books that support the existence of Christ; unfortunately, they have mostly been lost or are simply not reliable. Notably, there was Thallus, a historian we know very little of but who, in his book *History*, writes of an earthquake and great darkness, similar to what the New Testament mentions when Jesus was crucified. *Acts of Pilate* is allegedly an official document from Pontius Pilate and mentions an account of Jesus; unfortunately,

---

10. Translated by Alfred John Church and William Jackson Brodribb.
11. F. F. Bruce, *The New Testament Documents: Are They Reliable?* (Downers Grove, IL: InterVarsity Press, 2003), 117.

this text was most likely written by Christians and is not authentic. There is also Celsus, whose work did not survive; however, it is known that he wrote a document that attacked the Christian faith. He believed Jesus was merely a magician and sorcerer, but it's of important note because he acknowledged that Jesus existed and performed what Christians call miracles and what he called trickery.

The question is not whether Jesus Christ actually existed—it's whether he was who he said he was.

So that was quite a bit of information. Let me pause and lay it out briefly one more time—this time as a PowerPoint presentation:

Slide One—A giant word art smashes on the slide using a fancy turning-type animation. When you get over how awesome the animation was, you realize it says, "Age of Enlightenment." But before you can take that in, images of Newton, Spinoza, and Voltaire flash on the slide. Voltaire, with his sexy, long, flowing hair, is of course the best-looking of the bunch. Spinoza looks a little like a stoner, and Newton looks constipated.

Slide Two—An image of Friedrich von Thun, who played Albert Schweitzer in *The Young Indiana Jones Chronicles*, dances across the slide until it finds its place appropriately in the center. Von Thun is slightly more fetching than the real Schweitzer and is a much better selection for the slide. The image fades out and Schweitzer's book, *The Quest for the Historical Jesus*, appears in its place.

Slide Three—Text comes onto the slide with a seesaw effect. It reads "Myth Theory." Below it, three pictures appear. The first is a poorly illustrated stick figure drawing of Christians creating a man; the second is another poorly drawn image of

what may or may not be Jesus, and who is definitely not performing miracles; and finally, there are several questionable
stick figures which all look the same—clearly a weak effort
to show a weak theory.

Slide Four—We see a picture of a man I thought was Jaleel
White (who played Steve Urkel on *Family Matters*) standing in front of a camera shop at Disneyland. It turned out it
wasn't him.[12]

Slide Five—Two photos of a marble bust appear on the slide.
One is the younger and more dapper looking Josephus, and
the other is the older Suetonius.

Slide Six—This last slide shows the text "You can download
this presentation here: . . ." Curiously, no website is provided.

The year after *The Passion of the Christ* was released, during
Easter, my grandma came over and insisted we watch it again as
a family so we could experience the cruel torture of Jim Caviezel
together. What better way to celebrate Jesus rising from the dead than
to watch a movie that only vaguely references the fact that he did?

I heard a pastor explain how the movie really showed what Jesus
went through. So I tried to watch it the second time and do my best
to understand it.

No good.

I did not need to know the sheer amount of pain Jesus endured
on the way to the cross, and even if I did want to know, no movie—
or anything else—could effectively convey that. The pain he experienced was not something we were meant to feel. He experienced
it so we wouldn't have to. No amount of sensory detail could help

---

12. Whoops—I'm not sure how that slide got in there. My apologies.

me know just how much he suffered. What mattered to me was that he was a man—the God-man.

I believe that for many of us there are two Jesuses. There's the one we know as a child or teenager—the one who does awesome things, says awesome things, and is worthy of a t-shirt.

Then there's the Jesus we know as an adult. He's the one who says we have to go to church on Sunday. The problem with the second one is that if we don't take the time to know him, we'll most likely stop listening to him. Maybe we won't stop believing in him, but we'll certainly stop thinking about him.

In college I didn't think much about the historical Jesus (perhaps because I couldn't get past the image of old dudes throwing around colored beads). As I searched for Jesus as an adult, however, I wondered why it is so important to know who Jesus is outside the Bible.

To kids, Jesus seems almost magical: he's walking on water, raising dead people, changing water to wine, and so on. When you believe in someone like that, you'll probably eventually realize that you are believing in an X-Men character, not a Savior. Then you become an adult, and you believe he is real because—well, just because.

But when you believe in something "just because," it doesn't take much to knock the faith right out of you.

The New Testament tells us there was a man parading around doing some pretty fantastic things. Then when you strip away the Bible and ask, "But who was Jesus really?" what you find is multiple historic books and documents that also say there was a man parading around doing some pretty fantastic things.

For thousands of years, people lived in the dark—and not just because they didn't have electricity, though that didn't help. They accepted what ministers told them because they didn't have much choice. Mostly what they believed then was close to what we believe today, but sometimes it went a little off course.[13]

---

13. The most famous were the Gnostics, who believed they possessed a secret knowledge of Jesus. To a lesser extent, during the medieval period, legends emerged of dog-headed characters (a belief known as *cynocephaly*).

Then came the Age of Enlightenment, and now we live in a world of doubt. And doubting is a good thing. The Bible is full of doubters—and God loves the doubter as much as he loves believers.

If ever there was a person who should have doubted God, it was David.[14] He spent most of his life on the run, knowing death could find him at any moment. In Psalm 88, perhaps his gloomiest psalm, David concludes, "Darkness is my closest friend." That psalm is one of the strongest examples of a person doubting; David is in a bad place, and he cries his frustrations and doubts out to God. That's exactly what God wants.

The disciples were the biggest doubters of them all. Thomas doubted that Jesus rose from the dead until he could put his fingers through the holes in his hands that the nails had made. Peter, earlier in Jesus's ministry, was able to actually walk on water—until he started to doubt and then sank. Just before Jesus was arrested, it was Peter again who swore up and down he would not disown him—Peter was sure his faith was that strong. But he ended up denying he even knew Jesus three times.

Faith is restored in doubt.

The quest to rediscover Jesus—or perhaps discover him for the first time—should begin with doubt. God can take doubt. If anything is true, then it holds up against all doubt and reveals its true nature. What God can't take is the doubt that comes naturally, and the questioning that doesn't follow. It's in our nature to doubt; when we ignore doubt and believe in spite of what is inside us, then our guard is dropped and we put ourselves at risk of losing everything.

God is fine with my stripping apart Jesus. He's fine with my saying, "Jesus is real—but I'm not too sure about those miracles." He's fine with that because this isn't the last chapter, not the end of the journey; the quest continues to seek Jesus's true nature and understand—truly understand—not only who Jesus is, but why we should believe in him.

---

14. Of David and Goliath fame.

Getting Social

Twitter: Watch *The Passion of the Christ* and live tweet your commentary with the hashtag #passionoftheJew.

Pinterest: Pin every film portrayal of Jesus you can find.

Instagram: Hug your closest Jewish friend and say, "It's not your fault." Then ask to pose for a picture and post it on Instagram with the hashtag #itsnotyourfault.

LinkedIn: Add the church play/musical you did in grade school to your list of previous employers. Bonus points if said play was a passion play. If you were not in a church play or musical, then you can sit this response out.

Facebook: Find embarrassing photos of your friends and family in church plays. Post the photos and tag them.

WhichBibleHero AreYou?

What is your dream job?

- A. Writer and/or musician (+1)
- B. Politician (+3)
- C. To run the family business (+5)
- D. CEO (+7)
- E. Meteorologist (+9)
- F. Anything that carries the risk of death and lets me live on the wild side (+11)

Will the Real Jesus Please Step Up?

#AuthenticChrist

SHARE

Several years ago, an otherwise normal-looking man came to the library where I worked. He was dressed professionally, spoke intelligently, and smelled of expensive cologne. He was looking for books on writing cover letters.

His name was Messiah. He was, in his words, looking for a "career change."

I figured he was being sarcastic—that he would make some bizarre joke about no longer wanting to be the Son of God. He didn't. He actually no longer wanted to work in real estate and was hoping to find something better in sales or marketing.

He did go on to tell me that he realized he was the Messiah after receiving a vision. Everything else about the man was completely sane. He just had a bit of a Messiah complex.

Was he the Messiah? No. Did he think he was? Without a doubt.

The point is, anyone can say they are the Messiah. And anyone can believe it. Jesus existed! Great! But how can we really be sure he was the true Messiah?

Let's play a game of *Jeopardy*. For $400: He came from Galilee, his actions are mentioned in the Acts of the Apostles, he had many followers, and he was a great leader.

"Who is Jesus?"

Try again.

For $500, the correct answer is: "Who is Judas of Galilee?"[1]

Judas wasn't alone. Lots of people have claimed to be the Messiah—thousands, actually. There's probably some crazy guy who visits your own local library who thinks he is the Messiah. What is it that separates Jesus Christ from the library Christ who yells at the person behind the reference desk about his divine nature being stripped from him because the library refuses to allow him access to porn sites?

It's easy to believe in Christ, but if we want a rock-solid foundation of faith, then we have to actually *know* him, not just know *of* him. We have to know why his messianic claims were more valid than anyone else's.

Who do Jews say he is? And why don't they believe that Christians believe in the real Messiah? Can you really just pick and choose Bible verses to make up the Messiah? Do Jews even believe the Messiah will look anything like the Christian Messiah? What does it even mean to be the Messiah?

---

1. Probably not the Judas you're thinking of. This Judas walked around about the same time as Christ, led a revolt against the Romans, was mentioned by the historian Josephus in *Jewish Wars* and *Antiquities of the Jews*, and was considered by many at the time to be the Jewish Messiah. He was so important that the Bible also mentions him in Acts 5:37.

I believe that George Clooney is an actor. I know it because I see him in magazines, and I see his movies.[2] I can put my life on the line, I believe so strongly that George Clooney is an actor.

But Christ? How can I really put my life on the line for that guy? Because I read some book from thousands of years ago where he makes claims and supposedly does miracles? There was no film crew taking pictures of him; there are no YouTube videos of Jesus walking on water. So I'm essentially taking the word of people who were supposedly eyewitnesses. But there were also eyewitnesses to Buddha, to Muhammad, to lots of people. Were witnesses of Christ more accountable and less likely to exaggerate?

In order to say something like, "For to me, to live is Christ and to die is gain,"[3] I need a little more security in my faith than what simply taking a bunch of people's word for it can provide.

In college, I took a course in Buddhism. The first day of class, the professor went over the syllabus and his expectations of the students; when he was done, he said, "Are there any questions?"

A young student nearly knocked over his desk in excitement as he eagerly raised his hand in a "Pick me! Pick me!" sort of way.

The professor nodded at him. "Yes?"

The student actually stood to ask his question. I'm not sure why. He cleared his throat and asked, "Isn't it true that Jesus studied Tibetan Buddhism before he began his public ministry?" He then crossed his arms and waited for his answer.

The professor looked at him curiously. "I meant about the course—but since you asked, no, I do not believe that is true."

"I've read books on the subject!" the student protested passionately.

---

2. I even remember seeing him on *The Facts of Life* and *The Golden Girls*.
3. Philippians 1:21.

"And I'm sure they're page-turners," the professor said, smiling, "but there's simply no concrete evidence to support that. It's just a bunch of theories."

"And this is your opinion?"

"Of course."

He didn't sit for several seconds, which made both the class and the professor nervous. Finally he scratched his chin and quietly mumbled, "I see."

The student was quiet the rest of the class and never returned. He left a lasting impression on me—not just because he said something I had never heard before, but because it was my first exposure to some of the truly crazy stuff people say about Christ.

You know Christ is important because there are more stories and myths made up about him than anyone else. You don't hear crazy stories about Muhammad or Buddha or Confucius or any number of other great leaders in history.

With so many stories about Christ, it's important to recognize the truth from the fiction.

Let's take a step back. Okay, now let's take a few thousand more and let's look at a history of the Messiah claims. First, let's look at where the term comes from.

The word *messiah* literally means "anointed." That's a pretty broad term, and it's used quite a bit in the Old Testament. Lots of people, after all, are anointed.

David was anointed king over Israel, and under his leadership, the Jews had it pretty good, but it didn't take long for things to go sour for the Jewish people. They were soon conquered, and Jewish prophets began prophesying that another anointed leader would come to restore their rule. Unlike the Messiah that Christians believe in, this Messiah would not be God. He would come from the line of David and be a great leader, but his leadership would be more in the earthly and worldly sense of the word.[4] The period in which the Messiah will come is known in Judaism as the Messianic Age.

Jesus came from the line of David. Is it so hard to believe that he is the Messiah? Why do the Jewish people reject him? Because, in a nutshell, he didn't make Israel great again. Essentially, Jews regard Jesus as a false prophet. A prophet, according to Jewish tradition, would not free people from following Jewish law.

There were Jews who strongly disagreed with this idea, which is why most early Christians were regarded as simply Jews who belonged to a cult.[5]

Who were some of the other people that were once (and in some cases still are) considered to be the Messiah?

The first person widely regarded as a Messiah candidate lived nearly two hundred years before Jesus.[6] His name was Judas Maccabaeus. (If the name is vaguely familiar, then you might be Catholic or Orthodox or Coptic; those faiths hold the books of Maccabees to be canonical and include them in their version of the Old Testament.) Maccabaeus was considered to be the Messiah by some because he led a successful revolt and helped free the Jews from a foreign power.

A candidate who came just a few years before Jesus, Athronges, actually claimed to be the Messiah. Like King David, he was a shepherd. He led a revolt against the Romans, but he was defeated, and his Messiah dreams were crushed.

During the first century, when Jesus came, there were five other major Messiah figures on the scene. It was a time of unrest for the Jews, who constantly clashed with the Romans. Several Jewish leaders led revolts. Tensions eased a little after the first century, and

---

4. In other words, the kind of command-and-conquer leader who would make Israel great again.
5. Yes, Christians, your entire faith stems from a "cult."
6. By "candidate," I do not mean to imply he was accepted as the Messiah. Rather, people speculated that this could have been the case, even if it was later proven false.

there weren't quite as many revolts, which also meant there weren't as many Messiah candidates.

The most recent person to be widely considered a Messiah candidate is the late Menachem Mendel Schneerson (1902–1994). One of the greatest modern Jewish leaders, Schneerson made tremendous contributions to education and was beloved by thousands of followers. To his credit, he himself never claimed to be the Messiah.

Of all the people who claimed to be or were thought to be the Messiah, only Jesus has established a large following, and only Jesus's followers had substantial biblical prophecy to back up these claims.[7]

Christians and Muslims both agree that Jesus is the Messiah; interpretation differs, however, on what exactly this means. Christians believe he is the Son of God; Muslims believe he was the anointed leader and a great prophet. Both believe he will return to earth and defeat the Antichrist. Curiously, the person whom Jews will most likely hold as their Messiah will be the one Christians view as the Antichrist.

SHARE

WikiBreak

There have been several credible (for lack of a better word) Messiah candidates. But the truly fun ones are the ones who have been just a little bit . . . crazy.

Jones Very was on the original who's who list of Transcendentalism. He was Harvard educated, a scholar, a poet, and had the respect of people like Ralph Waldo Emerson. And then he went sort of nuts. He became convinced that he was the second coming of Christ. He continued teaching until he was institutionalized. He spent the remainder of his life refusing to renounce his belief.

Throughout the 1940s and 1950s, a cult known as Wisdom, Knowledge, Faith, and Love Fountain of the World (WKFL) in Simi Valley, California, became quite the trendsetter. Its followers were

---

7. Even if followers of Judaism believe that such use is misinterpretation of prophecy.

hippies, back when hippies weren't even cool yet. Members dressed in robes and walked around barefoot, and they surrendered all their income to the cult. Unlike some cults, they actually did help people. But that did not make up for the fact that their leader, Krishna Venta, was crazy, believing that he was Christ. Former members called bull in 1958. They suicide-bombed Venta, claiming he was misappropriating the cult's funding and getting it on with their wives.

Jesus was all about love, but apparently some believe he was about murder too. Thomas Provenzano killed or injured several people and believed that he was being executed because he was Jesus—not because he killed a bunch of people. Another convicted murderer, Maurice Clemmons, believed he was Christ, but he took it up a notch by claiming his wife was Eve. Clemmons also believed he came from a highly respected family: his brothers were LeBron James and President Obama, and his sister was Oprah Winfrey.

Nineteenth-century Mormon sect leader Arnold Potter thought he was Jesus and even nicknamed himself "Potter Christ." In 1872, fully convinced of his messianic powers, he told his followers in Council Bluffs, Iowa, that it was time for him to ascend to heaven. They followed him to the top of the bluffs, from whence he launched himself off the cliff—and instead of ascending, descended to his death.

Insanity runs high with Mormon sects. Another Latter-day Saint, William W. Davies, broke away from the church, believing that he was the archangel Michael. He never believed he was Christ; he was humble enough to save that role for his son, who was called "Walla Walla Jesus." Unfortunately for Davies, his son died young, and Davies's followers slowly began going away, realizing that Davies's visions were wrong.

If followers of Judaism don't think Jesus is the Messiah because he wasn't a political leader, then why do Christians think he is? What does the Bible say that makes so many people believe Jesus was indeed the Messiah?

Deuteronomy 18:15 is seen by most as the earliest Messiah prophecy: "The Lord your God will raise up for you a prophet like me from among you, from your fellow Israelites. You must listen to him."

The obvious problem with this verse and several other messianic verses is that it's a little vague. Could it describe Jesus? Of course! But it could also describe a lot of other people. In Isaiah, though, the prophecies become more specific. For example, Isaiah 53:5 says, "He was pierced for our transgressions, he was crushed for our iniquities; the punishment that brought us peace was on him, and by his wounds we are healed."

That certainly sounds like Jesus, who came and died for our sins. Jewish scholars beg to differ, saying that verse really is a reference to the Jewish people's suffering. But other prophets also had a lot to say about the Messiah. Micah 5:2 says, "But you, Bethlehem Ephrathah, though you are small among the clans of Judah, out of you will come for me one who will be ruler over Israel, whose origins are from of old, from ancient times." To a Christian, that of course means the Messiah will be born in Bethlehem, Jesus's birthplace, according to the gospels of Matthew and Luke.

Zechariah 9:9 says, "Rejoice greatly, Daughter Zion! Shout, Daughter Jerusalem! See, your king comes to you, righteous and victorious, lowly and riding on a donkey, on a colt, the foal of a donkey." That's exactly how all four of the gospels report that Jesus entered Jerusalem toward the end of his earthly ministry.

Zechariah 12:10 says, "I will pour out on the house of David and the inhabitants of Jerusalem a spirit of grace and supplication. They will look on me, the one they have pierced, and they will mourn for him as one mourns for an only child, and grieve bitterly for him as one grieves for a firstborn son." The gospel of John points to this prophecy as fulfilled when Jesus's side was pierced at his crucifixion (John 19:34).

Here are some other examples of prophecies fulfilled by Jesus.

Isaiah 7:14—"Therefore the Lord himself will give you a sign: The virgin will conceive and give birth to a son, and will call him Immanuel."

Isaiah 53:3—"He was despised and rejected by mankind, a man of suffering, and familiar with pain. Like one from whom people hide their faces he was despised, and we held him in low esteem."

Zechariah 11:12–13—"I told them, 'If you think it best, give me my pay; but if not, keep it.' So they paid me thirty pieces of silver. And the Lord said to me, 'Throw it to the potter'—the handsome price at which they valued me! So I took the thirty pieces of silver and threw them to the potter at the house of the Lord." According to tradition, Jesus was betrayed by Judas for thirty pieces of silver.

Isaiah 53:7—"He was oppressed and afflicted, yet he did not open his mouth; he was led like a lamb to the slaughter, and as a sheep before its shearers is silent, so he did not open his mouth." Mark 15:4–5 reports that Jesus was silent before his accusers.

Isaiah 53:12 says he would be killed with transgressors (i.e., criminals)—"Therefore I will give him a portion among the great, and he will divide the spoils with the strong, because he poured out his life unto death, and was numbered with the transgressors. For he bore the sin of many, and made intercession for the transgressors."

Could some of these be just a poor reading of the text? Sure, why not. Could some be from a bad translation? It's possible. But here's the thing: this is just a tiny sampling of fulfilled prophecy—all written hundreds of years before Jesus came. Most Christian scholars hold that *more than three hundred* biblical prophecies were fulfilled by Jesus Christ.

It's harder to claim prophecy has been misrepresented when so many prophecies are involved.

So what about the Jews? What about their false teacher argument: that a true teacher would never claim to be God and would not teach what is essentially abandonment of the Mosaic Law? Are Christians really just worshiping an idol, as followers of Judaism would say?

Jews will agree with this: things in the Bible rarely happen as we expect. When messianic prophecy was riding high, the Jewish people were riding low. So why not expect such prophecy to mean that a person was going to come and restore them? Makes sense to me! That is how humans think. But it's not how God thinks.

Although God established his reign on earth through his chosen people, the Jewish people, it was never his plan to be the God of just one people and one nation. God was setting up shop through his first covenant; then Christ came to unleash God on all people.

However, the Jews knew that only God could abolish the law of the first covenant and ordain a new covenant for man. If a man in ancient Israel had come and said, "Hey, guess what? God's not just for the Jews, he's for everyone!" he would have carried no authority. Had a prophet made the attempt, he would have been considered a false teacher.

> ### USELESS POLL
>
> **Jesus is the real deal because . . .**
> A. my pastor says so.
> B. I've spent a great amount of time investigating his life and find there's no other conclusion.
> C. he just feels right.
> D. my mom and dad said there'd be no Christmas if he wasn't real. I really like Christmas.
>
> To be part of this poll, visit:
> www.OrganicJesus.com/useless-polls

Did Jesus think he was God? Did he say so? That's a popular topic for some scholars. Entire books have been written suggesting it was all a misunderstanding and Christ never actually said he was God.

So—did he?

Sometimes the Gospels seem a little vague on whether Jesus actually said he was God. He never stands on a mountain and yells, "I am God!" Apparently that's what some scholars believe he needed to do to be considered God. But there's a problem with that thinking: it's not something God would have done!

So what *did* Jesus say? Here are a few of his statements worth considering.

> John 10:30—"I and the Father are one." That certainly got the Jewish audience fuming!

> John 8:58—"Before Abraham was, I am" (NRSV). In case you need a little refresher, "I am" is how God referred to himself in the Old Testament. It was the name by which God identified himself to Moses: When the Israelites asked who sent him, God told Moses, "Tell them I am sent you" (see Exod. 3:14). Jesus used that same identifier in the New Testament. Things got heated at the temple when Jesus said, "Before Abraham was born, I am!" (John 8:58).

> Luke 22:30—"So that you may eat and drink at my table in my kingdom and sit on thrones, judging the twelve tribes of Israel." That's a pretty mighty thing for a man to say. What mere man has a kingdom in heaven?

> Matthew 28:18—"All authority in heaven and on earth has been given to me." Again, the authority Jesus claimed for himself far exceeded that of an ordinary man.

> Luke 6:5—"The Son of Man is Lord of the Sabbath." (See also Matt. 12:8 and Mark 2:28.) Why is this important? Because in Genesis, God said that the Sabbath was his. How can Jesus claim to be Lord of something that is God's without saying he is God?

Some have said that only in the gospel of John does Jesus allude to himself as divine. But that's obviously not true. We've just looked at a few of the places in *all* of the Gospels where Jesus claims to be God. There are many more.

In case you missed it, Jesus didn't die for being a good guy. Jesus died because he claimed to be God. That's inarguable; the Gospels, all of them, are clear about it.

Furthermore, all the early Christians certainly believed in both his divine nature and the nature of the Trinity. The letters of the New Testament make that plain. Jesus's divine nature wasn't something whipped up by Christians a few hundred years later; it was believed from the get-go.

Why was Jesus so vague, then? He wasn't; the Jewish leaders certainly didn't think he was. They heard him loud and clear. Still he could have said, "I'm God" just once, no? But again, that doesn't seem to be God's nature. He tells you enough for you to draw that conclusion, but ultimately, it's your choice whether to embrace it.

Ultimately, you'll find evidence enough for Christ's divinity, but it's not in his nature to hand it to you without letting you work it out for yourself. Being on fire for God comes from certainty of belief, and he wants people on fire, not just sort of smoking. It was never the no-brainer choice that some Christians make it out to be; Jesus wanted his followers to grasp his true nature on their own.

One thing that separates Jesus from the religious type you've seen on TV—the evangelist who dazzles and amazes—is that Jesus never used trickery. And he never used pressure to force decisions; he never said, "Believe or go to hell!" Jesus understood how humans process. He knew that we need to work through things in order to believe.

A lot of people think Jesus was a great preacher. If you are a Christian and you think that—well, good. I would hope you do. But if you're *not* a Christian and you believe that, then perhaps you should think more deeply. Jesus claimed to be God. Great teachers don't make that claim—unless it's true. I can think of a lot of great preachers, but if they ever said they were God, then their credibility with me would vanish.

So perhaps the most pressing question for you isn't whether Jesus was the Messiah. For you it may be, Can you invite God into your heart and mind to let you work through the process of belief?

Getting Social

Twitter: Link to a story about a person who claims to be Jesus: #unrealJesus.

Pinterest: Create a board called "Seriously?" that's full of clippings of various books and websites about people who have claimed to be Jesus.

Instagram: Take a picture of a statue or painting that represents Jesus: #trueMessiah.

LinkedIn: Search LinkedIn for people who list Messiah as a job skill; share your results on Twitter or Facebook.

Facebook: Share a story about a person who claims to be Jesus. Bonus points: Don't reply to anyone who comments.

Which Bible Hero Are You?

Which book would you most likely be reading?

A. *Leaves of Grass* by Walt Whitman (+1)

B. *Schindler's List* by Thomas Keneally (+3)

C. *Horton Hatches the Egg* by Dr. Seuss (+5)

D. *How to Win Friends and Influence People* by Dale Carnegie (+7)

E. *The Circus of Dr. Lao* by Charles G. Finney (+9)

F. *The Adventures of Huckleberry Finn* by Mark Twain (+11)

Chapter Three

Does God Have a Pinky Toe?

#ChristianEvolution

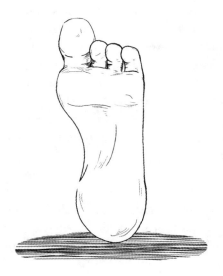

From a purely lyrical perspective, Peter J. Peters was pretty awesome; his name just flows off your lips. Unfortunately, Peter (or Peters, as he was formally known) let that awesome name go to his head. He was like that cranky old neighbor who hated

53

everyone—only he was worse than that. He didn't stop at hating those darn skateboarders with their loud music; he also hated Jews and lots of other people. He kind of made former Westboro Baptist Church pastor Fred Phelps look like a warm, fuzzy, and gentle soul. Peters first came to national attention in the 1980s when several people who had attended his church were found to be connected to everything from firebombing buildings to even murder.

There was one more thing about Peters. He is said to have believed in lizard people. No joke.

It's easy to pass him off as just one of those crazy Christians we aren't supposed to take seriously.

Here's the problem: people *do* take them seriously.

There comes a point in every Christian's life when he or she has to look around and say, "Am I the crazy one?" When you see a religion full of people like Peters, how can you not?

My search for the Organic Jesus was more than a journey to get to the historical roots of Christianity. It was a search to discover if belief was even tangible—if one could be a well-grounded person and still believe in something that, from a purely scholarly level, makes absolutely no sense.

You'd really be crazy not to wonder if you were crazy for believing. Some ministers even give sermons on how crazy Christians are, the argument being that Christianity is a religion composed of ideas that are not in the natural instincts or behaviors of man, so it is therefore crazy to believe them—and it is this belief in the crazy that makes Christians so . . . special.

Maybe someone telling you that you are crazy is just what you need—but maybe it's not what you need. Religion—any religion—is not based on tangible ideas that you can prove; it's based on faith. If it were not based on faith, then it would be called history.

But there has to be logic to faith. Peter writes in 1 Peter 3:15 that we should always be prepared to give a reason for the hope that we have. Buddhism, Hinduism, Islam—they can all make you feel warm and fuzzy. So why follow Christianity over any of them? Does Christianity make you feel more warm and fuzzy?

If Peter was right—if we do have to be prepared to give a reason for the hope that we have—then there has to be something more than feelings. Yet when I look around, what I see is people who base their faith in Christ more on a feeling than on truth. Feelings can give you the relationship you need with Christ, but truth can give you the confidence to believe that relationship is real.

The problem with feelings is not the warmth you feel in good times; it's the coldness you feel in the dark times. When bad things come your way—and they will—you will question if those feelings were ever real to begin with or if you were just crazy, and you will have no truth to keep your faith strong.

> **USELESS POLL**
>
> **Evolution proves . . .**
> A. nothing.
> B. that science can be used to show that an intelligent designer is at work.
> C. that science is just code for liberal propaganda.
> D. Both A and C are correct.
>
> To be part of this poll, visit:
> **www.OrganicJesus.com/useless-polls**

My greatest doubt in God has come by looking at other Christians—looking at them and thinking, "If this is who believes in God, then can there really be a God?" I have often found myself in a room full of Christians who love only one thing greater than *Duck Dynasty*, and that is football. These people are my brothers and sisters in Christ, but where does that leave me? When I look around and it seems that the most powerful defendant of my faith is Kirk Cameron, it's easy to wonder, "Is it all a fairy tale?"

I don't want to believe because I'm crazy. I want to believe because it's true. I want to believe because in my perfectly sane state, I can see the presence of God.

Jesus teaches in Matthew 7:26–27 that people who hear his words but do not act on them are like people who build their homes on sand; the rain comes and the house is knocked over. Jesus is speaking about people who want the feeling, people who came to see him because they want the miracle—because they want that warm, fuzzy feeling.

What these people just don't get—what a lot of people don't get—is that when faith and truth work together, you become unstoppable.

We live in a world where we don't have to believe—a world where there are answers for many of the questions and problems of the universe. It is a unique time and we will be defined by it.

I don't believe I've ever heard of a modern theologian saying they were doing groundbreaking work; for the most part, it's all been studied. People will certainly continue to say old things in a fresh new way to keep the study contemporary, but that doesn't change the fact that, barring an archaeological discovery to blow us all out of the water, Christian theology is probably not going to change very much.[1] Science, in contrast, is exciting. New discoveries are made almost daily if not hourly. It's a good time to be a scientist.

One of the problems I saw arising as I grew in my faith is a giant misconception that science and God do not mix—that if we have God, then we have to throw things like evolution out the window; that if there are any theories that even remotely set out to interrupt your belief, then you just have to slap a giant "invalid" across them. There are so many Christians out there who reject completely tangible and logical ideas simply because they are fearful of understanding them.

Curiously, there are just as many non-Christians who reject completely tangible and logical Christian ideas simply because they are fearful of understanding them. The fact is, some non-Christian scientists can be just as intellectually irresponsible as some Christian scientists. If Christ came today—if he did miracles and even raised people from the dead—many scientists would just get angry, shrug their shoulders, and say, "Well that's just great. God just set back scientific progress by two thousand years by giving people hope."

A few years ago, a friend said to me, "You seem pretty well-read. You went to school; you studied religion; you're open minded. How can you believe in God?"

---

1. Which isn't to say we should abandon the field of study; it only means our field will grow at a much slower pace than science.

I thought for a minute, then said, "Is there something out there—some field of study—that proves there is no God?"

"Not that I'm aware of."

"Then I believe because there's nothing that proves otherwise." I paused a moment and then asked, "But let me ask you the same thing: You've studied science. You're a smart person. How much time have you invested in actually seeing if there is something out there?"

"Not a lot."

It was interesting how much he believed that a Christian could not be intelligent—that as soon as thought came into the picture, God was thrown out the window. At what point in history did that happen? At what point did believing in God mean you couldn't have any remote form of intelligence?

There are certainly plenty of smart Christians, but lately, it seems they are more of the underdogs. There's a bias in the scientific community against Christians, but it has more to do with Christians who arrogantly reject new ideas of science than because scientists are evil, stubborn people who are too proud to accept there could be a Creator. In fact, between 1901 and 2000, 65.4 percent of all Nobel Prize Laureates have identified, in part, as Christian; over 70 percent in the field of chemistry; over 65 percent in the field of physics; and 62 percent in the field of medicine. The field with the lowest percentage of Christians? Economics—which has absolutely nothing to do with science.[2] Are there scientists with bias? Of course. But that doesn't mean scientists, by and large, are out to get everyone.

When Christians today hear the word *science*, many of them almost instantly think of evolution. Christians have spent the past several years trying to say there's a mass conspiracy to hide the beliefs of well-known creationists, while atheists have used creationism as fuel to stoke their growing fire.

God uses all things to serve his purpose. That includes evolution.

---

2. Baruch Aba Shalev, *100 Years of Nobel Prizes* (Los Angeles, CA: Americas Group, 2002).

There is absolutely no reason why God cannot have created a species that evolved to meet the conditions of its environment. Further,
there is absolutely no reason why kids cannot hear different theories
about how life began. Does that mean evolution is true? No. Does
that mean it's false? No. Evolution is not a fact; it's a theory. And it's
a theory that continues to evolve today as scientists (both Christian
and non-Christian) find holes in the theory or expand on it.

Much of the reason people lose faith is because of how they were
sheltered as children. We are not raising children who can defend
themselves; we are creating children who need us in order to survive—a struggle for existence that is about survival not of the fittest, but of the fittest parent.

There's a horrible mentality that it's us against them. That we
have to stand up against scientists because they are out to get us. But
if we stop barging into science and forcing our belief system onto it,
then we might actually win the war that we are supposedly fighting.

Christians should not be teaching their children how to disprove
science; they should be teaching children how to appreciate it and
how to see God in it.

Not long ago I was having lunch with a fellow Christian. He mentioned that his church was having a creation scientist speak at his
church to discuss the threat of science in our schools. I have nothing
against a creation scientist; I'm sure they're nice, intelligent people—
but that word *threat* interested me. I asked, "So science is a threat?"

"Big time! You should hear what they're teaching the kids in
school. Global warming! Do you believe that? They're only in the
fourth grade and they're already polluting their minds."

"So creation science disproves global warming?"

"He's not just about creationism—he's about the whole conspiracy. Global warming is like a gateway to all the propaganda."

My point here isn't to prove or disprove global warming;[3] my point
is that a lot of Christians have tried to make it seem like we're losing
a war against science. But there is no war. There is no scientist sitting

---

3. But seriously: Study up! Your children are depending on it.

in a room trying to figure out how to destroy Christianity—at least not one that I'm aware of. There are a few scientists out there who seem to make it their mission to make Christians angry, but for the most part scientists are nice people who have nothing against anyone.

The biggest thing working against Christianity isn't science—it's the fact that we live in a privileged society where belief is a right that cannot be taken away. Most Christians never have to worry about being persecuted, but some Christians still try to take something like science and say that they are indeed being persecuted—not by the sword, but by the mind of a scientist!

It's easy to see why there is so much prejudice toward Christians in the scientific community. Some Christians stand in the way of science for fear that science may disprove God or somehow hinder their faith. Science will never do that. There comes a point where we have to accept that if there is a God, then God can and will defend himself.

When Jesus was arrested, Simon Peter ran to his aid and cut off the ear of one of the soldiers. Jesus quickly healed the ear and rebuked Peter. It's one of God's greatest examples of how he doesn't need us rushing to his aid to defend his cause. God calls us to serve him by action—by love.

Oddly enough, what is often forgotten by Christians and by many modern scientists alike is the sheer amount of knowledge that they owe to Christian believers.

- Science would have no solar system without Galileo Galilei, who was famously condemned by the church only to be called, hundreds of years later, one of its greatest heroes.[4]
- Without Blaise Pascal, our iPhones would not have a calculator;[5] math and physics owe few other scientists more than

---

4. The Catholic Church banned Galileo's work in 1615, even though Galileo tried to defend himself and show how science only reinforced God. By the 1700s, the Catholic Church was willing to publish his work, though it was partially censored. By 1939, Pope Pius XII praised Galileo, and he's been a Catholic hero ever since.
5. Heck, even with Pascal, our iPads still don't have a built-in calculator. Come on, Apple!

they owe Pascal. Often overshadowed by his contributions to science were his contributions to Christianity. Pascal, in addition to his writings on science, wrote quite extensively on Christian philosophy.[6]

- Astronomy and physics often all come back to Isaac Newton. Newton was always quick to point out that all those things he saw in space were the creation of an intelligent designer.
- Genetics is one of the biggest topics in science today; understanding it could help cure mutations in our gene code that cause such horrible afflictions as cancer and cystic fibrosis. The father of genetics is a man by the name of Gregor Mendel—a great man, a great scientist, and a friar of the church. Yes, the man who is responsible for discovering that we have a genetic makeup was a Catholic priest.

The list of scientists of influence who were Christians goes on and on. It used to be that scientists would use their findings to show God's beauty in the universe.

Here's the dirty little secret about science: it does not disprove God. To think otherwise is like saying we can't study math because it disproves literature. They're two completely different schools of thought. They can live happily together.

Atheists sometimes try to use science to enhance their cause—to make Christianity[7] a mere fairy tale—but that's not science. That's using the same silly tactics some Christians have used for hundreds of years. Science is just a bunch of theories—some proven, some not. It's not threatening to faith. It can help prove faith if you let it. The reality is that God can take the thing you love and show you his power in it. If you love science, you can find God through it; if you love sports, you can find God; heck, if you love food, you can find God!

---

6. Also often overlooked was the fact that Pascal had a religious conversion later in life, and after that was on fire for Christ until his death.

7. Or any religion, for that matter.

Science is about the function of life, but faith is about its meaning; science can never explain our purpose for being.

Atheism has more to do with a rejection of Christianity than a rejection of God. Only in the past fifty years has the belief that there is no God really taken off. Why is that? What I find curiously sad is that some of the most famous atheists were hurt by Christianity in some way, whether by some kind of rejection or simply by bad teaching. I've heard many people say they abandoned faith when they asked the hard questions but did not get answers.

It would not be far off to say that Christianity contributed more to the rise of atheism than any other cause. Science did not create atheism—Christians did. Allow me to explain.

People don't fall from grace because they discover there's no truth to Christianity. Of course there are exceptions; there are always exceptions. But by and large, people fall because when they were children, they were fed a fairy tale. Fairy tales are nice for kids. But then we get older, and we learn the real story of the fairy tale—and there are some ugly truths behind it. And we aren't prepared for them. So we decide we were lied to.

We weren't lied to. The childhood story was true. But we need to be prepared for the arguments against it—and that means we need to hear the story in its entirety, including the ugliness. Otherwise, chances are someone else will tell us about the ugliness, and that person won't be a Christian; they'll be something else. And we'll believe that person because they were the only ones willing to share the ugly side with us.

I've heard a lot of Christian lectures that debate atheism; I don't recall any that talk about the valid points it raises. There's nothing wrong with talking about the opposing viewpoint. It only strengthens our own faith.

The fact is, the opposing argument is not very strong; most atheists will say something along the lines of, "If there is a God, then where is God? Where is God when a child dies? Where is God when there's a natural disaster? Where is God?"

So? Where is God? It's been two thousand years since God walked on earth through Christ. So what's up with that? God doesn't feel like doing wacky miracles anymore? Why does God feel so absent if he truly does exist?

Try this answer on for size: God shows up through you and me. Christ is God, and God is love, and since Christ lives in us, therefore so does love. God gives Christians this amazing way to show his presence to the world, and that is through love. But if we are too busy for people, then that love just won't come through. If you truly want to see the presence of God, go look for a Christian who forgives when he should hate; who helps when there is no benefit in it for her in helping. In short, go look for a Christian who follows Christ and not one who simply believes in him. People want proof of God, and God has empowered Christians to show his presence, but so many of us have fallen short.

WikiBreak

Charles Darwin is often viewed as the cherished saint of atheism, and as just plain evil by some Christians. And why not? He did, after all, write *On the Origin of Species*, which is classic, banned nonfiction for every good Christian.

Funny thing about Darwin: he wasn't an atheist. He spent most of his younger years attending church. There's wide debate on why he stopped, but he would admit only to being an agnostic. Darwin did his best throughout his life to separate religion and science, and he believed that the two could actually coexist.

But if not Darwin, then who? Who is the patron saint of atheism? It wasn't a scientist. It was a German philosopher by the name of Ludwig Feuerbach. One of Feuerbach's biggest fans was Karl Marx, who is himself the father of Communism.

Science really played no role in the birth of atheism. Christians standing in the way of scientific progress certainly did. I imagine it would be difficult to look at the complex workings of both the earth and the universe without coming away with a belief that some greater power had to have played a role.

The real culprits of atheism from its start, and still today, are philosophers, and yet most people are so busy arguing about whether science should or shouldn't be taught in school that they fail to see science was never really the problem.

As I searched for the Organic Jesus, I realized the only way to discover his true nature was to question everything—to build a faith that was surrounded not by a cute picket fence, but rather, by indestructible walls that could withstand whatever life tossed my way.

What's happened in this world is that we have evolved with scientific advances but Christianity has stayed the same. For thousands of years, Christians have been able to comfortably say, "God exists because God exists." But when the Age of Enlightenment came, logic began evolving. If you didn't want to believe in God, you could find reasons to support your atheism.

There's plenty to support the idea that God is alive and well. But when you look around, the arguments for him seem to appeal more to feelings than to logic. Sermons, books, movies—they all try to convince you based on feelings.

What bothered me as I matured in faith—as I started seeing it a little more organically—is how Christians sometimes can get a little . . . ritualistic. Not wanting to investigate science, for instance, because it doesn't support the way things have always been done. Not wanting to question theology because it might call into question hundreds of years of what was previously thought. If Christianity is declining, it has more to do with Christians closing the door—Christians saying, "Come on in," but meaning, "Leave that theology, belief, or behavior at the door."

That's not God talking; that's man talking. Transformation does not happen outside of church; it happens inside of church. It happens when people are let into the church and are able to see the power of God. If there is to be Christian renewal, then we have to let all people and beliefs in and let God transform their lives.

For Christians, there is one way to heaven, and that is Christ—
but from here, for many people, things get a little tricky. As long
as you conform to a certain value set, then you are good. If a man
cheats on his wife—forgivable. If a woman had an abortion ten
years ago, that's a little bit of a gray area for some Christians—it
is, at the very least, an area where we can get a little judge-y. Some
Christians, at some point in their lives, decide that because they
have read the Bible,[8] they are in the right mind-set to play God and
decide the salvation of others.

The Bible says one clear thing about what it takes for a Christian
to have salvation. It's a two-step program according to Romans
10:9:

1. Confess with your mouth that Jesus is Lord.
2. Believe in your heart that God raised him from the dead.

When Christ came, followers tended to be righteous; today it
seems that followers tend to be self-righteous. Christ did not say,
"Follow me, all who are not gay." Christ did not say, "Follow me,
all who have not murdered." Christ did not say, "Follow me, all who
have not cheated on your spouse." What *did* Christ say? He said,
"Follow me"—period. That can be difficult for some Christians
to hear, because it's much easier to believe what we have always
believed, and what our parents always believed, and what our
grandparents always believed, than to say that people are hurting,
and God loves them, and God wants them to follow him.

God wants us to love people without playing the role of God and
telling them they need to give up whatever we feel they are doing
wrong. God is God and we are not; a person's having a personal
relationship with God has absolutely nothing to do with us.

When you follow Christ—when you confess with your mouth
that Jesus is Lord and believe in your heart that God raised him

---

8. Or sometimes just because they have heard of the Bible and watched TBN.

from the dead—something amazing happens: you transform. If there is an area of your life that is wrong, then you will grow out of it. Christ forgives you in an instant, but transformation comes at a much slower pace.

Paul writes in Galatians 2:20 that he has been crucified with Christ and no longer lives, but Christ lives in him. What he means, applying his words to us, is that when we believe in Christ, we surrender ourselves to him. We let Christ lead our life. And a new life begins.

The Christian faith isn't so much a lifestyle as a journey. First Corinthians 10:23 says that everything is permissible, but not everything is beneficial. When someone believes in Christ, God is going to work with that man or woman on a spiritual journey—one that builds that person up. That's going to look different for each person. What's beneficial to one person is not necessarily beneficial to another.

I can only wonder what the world would look like if it was full of broken Christians—Christians who surrendered all and who admitted that they no longer lived but Christ lived in them.

Christianity isn't supposed to be about sharing the love of Christ with all those who share our values; Christianity is about welcoming those who put all our beliefs at risk and proving that love will always win.

Christianity will die if we don't let the broken in, if we don't open our arms to sinners and let God, not man, work in them to realize their potential. It is sad to think how many have turned from the cross because the church did not allow them to enter until they conformed to a certain "Christian" lifestyle.

The person who can have the greatest impact on Christianity isn't the jock who towers over everyone else and has incredible presence when entering a room. It isn't the debater who can debunk any argument. And it isn't the person who always brings real food to the potluck, not a bucket of cold KFC chicken.[9] It's the Christian

---

9. Though let's be honest, those people are awesome.

who's a little crazy—crazy enough to actually do the stuff that really counts.

It's a little crazy, for instance, to love your enemies—that doesn't make sense. And what about caring for someone when you'll get nothing in return? I don't get it. It's crazy. And that's okay. Bring on the crazies! What if we even took "crazy" to the next level? What if we started letting people in the doors who in the past wouldn't have been well received? What if the church—dare I say it—evolved?

The people of greatest impact in Christianity are the weak and brokenhearted, the people who surrender all, not because it just feels right but because they are hopeless and can only exist with God working through them. The people of greatest impact to Christianity come from the place you least expect it.

Getting Social

Twitter: Find an article about a scientific breakthrough or discovery and link to it with the hashtag #JesusIsScience.

Pinterest: Create a board called "Really?" full of clippings of various books and websites that try to prove science wrong because of fear that it might hurt Christianity. Need help getting started? Find a website about dinosaurs never existing. (Yes, these websites really exist, even though Christians by and large have absolutely no problem believing in dinosaurs.)

Instagram: Take a picture of your foot and ask your followers two things: (1) What is the pinky toe's purpose? and (2) Does God have a pinky toe? #ChristianEvolution.

LinkedIn: Find the people in your connections feed who are, in some form, a scientist. Endorse their skills.

Facebook: Share an article about a scientific breakthrough or discovery along with your thoughts on its findings. Bonus points: Don't reply to anyone who comments.

WhichBibleHero **Are**You?

Which person (real or fictional) would you most like to have a conversation with?

- A. William Shakespeare (+1)
- B. Martin Luther King Jr. (+3)
- C. Samwise Gamgee (+5)
- D. Abraham Lincoln (+7)
- E. Oscar Wilde (+9)
- F. Calamity Jane (+11)

ChapterFour

50 Shades of Bible

#BibleMyth

**Bible as a
Doorstop**

**Bible as a
Decoration**

**Bible as
Literature**

The Bible is a myth.

Shhh! Don't say that in church. Don't even tell your churchy friend. If you do you'll be labeled as one of "those people."

The underlying problem of the Bible myth theory stems from a misconception in how people perceive myth. Myths are nothing more than stories people tell to explain their history. The story of Robin Hood, for example, is told to explain a part of English history.[1] Does the fact that it's a myth mean the story is untrue? No. Does it mean the story is true? No.

So what does it mean? It means it's a myth!

When people talk about the "creation myth," they may be trying

---

1. You may know him as the popular, fictional Disney character. But while the Disney version may have taken a few creative liberties, there is historical evidence to suggest that there was a real Robin Hood.

to say they believe it is made up, but what they are really saying is that it's a story people tell to explain their origin. You can believe it's literally real, or you can believe it's metaphorically real.

For years, I believed that the Bible couldn't be a myth. How dare anyone even say so!

This changed during my junior year in college when I took a class appropriately titled "The Bible as Literature." It gave me an entirely new perspective on the Bible. I found myself spending hours in the library reading everything I could on the subject.

We hear a lot from preachers on the theology of the Bible and how it applies to our lives. If you spend a lot of time in front of the History Channel, then you probably hear a lot about the historical side of the Bible. Very rarely is there any discussion of the *literary* side of the Bible.

I find this incredibly odd, because when you open the Bible and start looking at the structure, you begin to see just how complex it really is. Beyond the stories, the theology, the prophecies, the commandments, beyond all of this, is a structure that is shaped almost like a mathematical puzzle.

What I've always found fascinating about the Bible is that the style of writing is just as good today as it was thousands of years ago. When I would read something like Beowulf, I appreciated it for its merits and its contribution to the literary narrative, but its dialogue and structure always seemed a little . . . bad. This has never been the case with the Bible. It never felt dated. It never felt poorly written. It never felt like any of the ancient classics. While it dealt with time periods vastly different from today, there was always a contemporary feel to it, regardless of which translation I was reading. The writing was truly ahead of its time—ahead of any time.

Starting with the beginning, the book of Genesis, a pattern immediately emerges. Creation is described, yes; but when you look at it more closely, the actual text is creating—each verse is building off the one that comes before it. You can see this by looking at the pattern that is found at the start of Genesis:

    a1. Light
        b1.   Sea and sky
            c1.   Dry land
    a2. Luminaries
        b2.   Fish and birds
            c2.   Land animals and humans
               d. Sabbath

Why is that important? Because each day is becoming greater and greater—the order in which it is described shows the earth progressively getting greater and greater. And the order of the first set matches the order of the next—so light happens first in the first set of days (a1), and luminaries (objects filled with light) come first in the next set (a2); sea and sky are mentioned next in the first set (b1); and what fills sea and sky? Fish and birds (b2).

The words it takes to describe these events also get progressively longer. This abcabcd pattern is very common in the Bible, but there are dozens of other patterns. All the stories in Genesis, for example, follow a symmetrical pattern. Let's look at just one story, that of Joseph:

    a. Introduction (Gen. 37:2–11)
      b. Grieving in Hebron (37:12–36)
        c. Reversal of the rights of elder and younger sons (38)
          d. Joseph's enslavement *to* Egyptians (39)
            e. Disfavor at Pharaoh's court (40)
              f. Joseph's revelation of Pharaoh's dream (41)
                g. Joseph's brothers come to Egypt for food (42)
                g. Joseph's brothers come to Egypt for food a second time (43:1–44:3)
              f. Joseph's revelation of his identity (44:4–45:15)

      e. Family sees how Joseph is favored in Pharaoh's
          court (45:16–47:12)

     d. Joseph's enslavement *of* Egyptians (47:13–26)

    c. Reversal of the rights of elder and younger sons
       (47:27–49:32)

   b. Grieving near Hebron (49:33–50:14)

 a. Conclusion (50:15–26)

You can see that Genesis wasn't written on a whim; there's complexity to each story. You can find these patterns all over Genesis. In fact, the entire Bible follows similar complex patterns that extend from book to book. Here's one for Genesis and Exodus:

 a. God's power in the creation account (Gen. 1–11)

   b. God promises numerous descendants and an exodus
      from slavery (12:1–21:7)

    c. Triumph of younger brother over older (21:8–28:4)

     d. Birth of the twelve tribes (28:5–37:1)

    c. Triumph of younger brother over older (37:2–50:26)

   b. God increases Israel in numbers and delivers them out of
     Egypt (Exod. 1:1–13:16)

 a. God's power in the desert (13:17–19:2)

I'll stop here, but there are literally hundreds and hundreds of similar patterns throughout the Bible—not just in the first books, but in every book.[2] When reading the Bible, most people just see what God says and reveals to his people. That's a good start. But if you really want to understand it, then look not just at what God reveals, but *how* he reveals it.

---

2. While researching this book, I used *The Literary Structure of the Old Testament: A Commentary on Genesis–Malachi* by David A. Dorsey (Grand Rapids: Baker, 1999) as a reference. This book discusses the Bible as literature in far greater detail than I ever could.

WikiBreak

SHARE

Let's look up a few favorite Bible passages that people like to share with friends:

"God helps those who help themselves."

"Hate the sin, love the sinner."

"Cleanliness is next to godliness."

"God works in mysterious ways."

Did you find them? Of course you didn't—because they aren't in the Bible. Some are Bible verses reimagined. Some are completely unbiblical. The point is, we sometimes have a way of just accepting things that should be scrutinized.

Curiously, people who get upset with the phrase "The Bible is a myth" frequently have no problem believing certain things are in the Bible that actually *aren't*. I'm sure you have seen movies about the exodus that show the Hebrews (or Jews) building the pyramids. It makes for a nice cinematic experience, but it's nowhere in the Bible.

And how can we ever forget the classic scene of Adam and Eve eating an apple? Easy. It doesn't say they ate an apple. They ate fruit. It could have been an apple—it could have been any one of a number of other things.

Oh, and what about the devil figure with horns and a pitchfork? Yeah! What about him? He's not biblical either.

The Bible isn't fiction. But you'd never know it by the stories we make up and say they're biblical—even though they're not.

When I completed my course on the Bible as literature, it was the first time that I really left a college course wanting more. I ended up doing an independent study with a mentor professor on the literary merits of the New Testament apocrypha.

Apocrypha is another word you don't say in church. The notion that there are other stories about Christianity is damning for some. Fictional books like *The Da Vinci Code* have only escalated the matter by leading people to believe that the church was hiding something from them—that secret documents existed to explain who Christ *really* was.

The truth is, the apocryphal texts have been around for a very long time (and never in hiding), almost as long as the New Testament—but not quite. The reason they weren't included in the New Testament wasn't because of what they said;[3] it had more to do with their dating. Dating has always been a matter of debate for scholars, but most would date the earliest apocryphal text around AD 200 or later. Some of the more popular apocryphal works were written 500 to 600 years after the death and resurrection of Jesus. That's why you don't see them in the Bible: church leaders agreed that they did not come from early Christians, and it would be too hard to validate what was true and what was not.

So if they aren't biblical, and they may or may not be true, and they weren't written by people with firsthand knowledge, then why should they be studied at all? Because of their mythical nature. They tell us profound things about the origins of Christianity— what early believers thought, how theology developed, and just how complex Christian notions actually are.

It's easy to listen to the pastor talk about the Bible and believe that Christianity, from its origins, was a pleasant little religion where there were no debates. But the apocryphal texts show us that was far from the case. Early Christians had lots of sects, just as there are today. Legends formed about the fathers of the church, some true, others not so much. Some were written to silence theological thought (if you didn't want a woman to speak, then just write about the legend you heard of Peter, who had something wise to say on the subject).

The assumption of Mary—the belief that Mary never died but rather was taken up to heaven—is a doctrine taught and believed by the Catholic Church. Its biblical foundation comes from Revelation

---

3. Some of them actually say profound things.

12; however, when we look at the apocrypha, we find a lot written about the assumption of Mary—it was a rather popular belief with the early church. So in this case, it can be said that we use the apocrypha to trace the origins of the belief. Is the doctrine true? Most Protestants would say no, but that's not to say it isn't.

Mary was a bigger figure in the New Testament apocrypha than in the Bible. The Protoevangelium of James (believed to be written around AD 145) tells of the childhood of Mary.

Many other books focus on the childhood of Jesus. And others talk about the acts of the first disciples. The Gospel of Judas shows that, while we may consider Judas a villain today, early Christians did not necessarily feel the same way; according to that writing, Judas receives forgiveness from God.

USELESS POLL

The Bible . . .
A. should be read, but who are we kidding? It's, like, super long!
B. is a myth.
C. is something I read when I need to fall asleep.
D. is something I read daily because it gives me hope in a world that can be hopeless.
E. Both B and D.

To be part of this poll, visit:
www.OrganicJesus.com/useless-polls

We can read the apocrypha and see things that may very well be true (legends usually begin with some truths, after all). However, we cannot read them as canonical truth because there's no way to separate the truth from the fiction.

When I finished my independent study, I was able to easily conclude that everything that's in the Bible should be in the Bible, and nothing should be added. But I also was able to conclude that there is relevance and even truth to the apocrypha.

The Bible is a myth, and I'm okay with that. For most of my life I've read the Bible, followed the Bible, and memorized the Bible. But when I realized it was a myth, the floodgates were opened. Suddenly there was surprisingly deeper dimensions to it. Most people admire the Bible at face value, and that's a shame. It's not just a great book with great wisdom; it's also a great book with a structure that is more complex than anything else ever written.

The priest led me to his dimly lit office, shut the door, switched on classical music, and sat behind his desk, tenderly studying my eyes. He was quiet for several seconds before he gave a long sigh and said, "Wouldn't it be great if there were a book about a Catholic priest who wants to have a romantic relationship with a nun, and they spend their entire lives fighting the temptation? And in the end nothing happens because they are too devoted to God? All fiction, of course."

The priest was an adviser for my final college thesis, and, despite his odd proposal for perhaps the most uninteresting book idea I had ever heard, he was quite resourceful in helping me understand that I wasn't alone. For some time I had begun to feel a little isolated. For four years I had been studying depressing modern and postmodern literature. For my final thesis, I would read nearly every major Christian work of fiction written in the past hundred years.

My junior year taught me that the Bible was much deeper and more complex than I once believed; my senior year taught me that, while the Bible may be the greatest book in Christianity's canon, there's plenty of supplemental material that can open your mind even more.

I told a friend about my senior thesis and he replied, with semi-disgust, "I love reading, but life is too short, and I only have time to read the Bible."

"Didn't you tell me just last week that you binge-watched *Gossip Girl*?"

"I said *read*."

"Of course you did."

But the point is, the Bible is the most important book for Christians, and yet there are hundreds of other books that can give new perspectives on its message and themes.

Recommended Reading

If you are looking for a good read, here is my list of some of the best Christian fiction from the past two hundred years.[4]

Contemporary Favorites

The Book of the Dun Cow by Walter Wangerin Jr.—If you like *Animal Farm* but are not quite into those pesky capitalist themes, then you'll love this animal fantasy. It's full of talking animals and overall awesomeness. For a more adult read, check out *Paul: A Novel*.

The Power and the Glory by Graham Greene—How can you not love a book whose main character is a deeply flawed, whiskey-drinking priest? Greene's works frequently touched on Catholic themes, but this book is by far one of his most thematic.

Wise Blood by Flannery O'Connor—I fell madly in love with O'Connor after reading this book. I'd have a poster-size picture of her in my office if only they made one. O'Connor isn't just one of the greatest Christian writers; she's one of the greatest writers. Her wit . . . her wisdom . . . they will deeply move you.

In the Beauty of the Lilies by John Updike—Updike is best known for the Rabbit series (and playing himself on an episode of *The Simpsons*). It's this book, however, that will rouse the interest of Christian readers. The epic novel covers four generations of a family and the decline of their Christian faith.

---

4. You can go further back and find even more, such as Dante's *Divine Comedy* and Milton's *Paradise Lost*. Also missing are contemporary favorites you already know or have heard of, like *The Screwtape Letters* or *A Wrinkle in Time*. If you are a serious reader, you've probably heard of some of the titles listed, but hopefully you will pick up one or two you haven't encountered.

Dwelling Places by Vinita Hampton Wright—Wright first burst grace-fully into the writing world with her novel *Grace at Bender Springs*. It's in this book, however, that Wright finds her voice. The novel proves that there is still a place for contemporary Christian literary fiction.

Classic Favorites

The next five books are in public domain in the United States (mean-ing you can download them for free). Grab a copy at your favorite online bookstore, or download a free copy at the links provided below.

In His Steps by Charles Sheldon—You've seen the WWJD (What Would Jesus Do) bracelets. Maybe you even have one. It's unfortu-nate that so many people have worn the bracelet but never both-ered with the unforgettable book. The message is just as relevant today as it was over a hundred years ago. www.OrganicJesus.com /in-his-steps

That Printer of Udell's by Harold Bell Wright—There was a time when Wright's name was as well known as Charles Dickens's. He was often cited as the first American to sell more than a million cop-ies of a book and make more than a million dollars from writing. His Christian themes have made him often forgotten. If you want to give him a try, start with this book, his first. www.OrganicJesus .com/that-printer-of-udells

A Voice in the Wilderness by Grace Livingston Hill—If you are a sucker for Christian romance novels, then try on this book for size. Actually, try on all of Hill's books for size. Hill, like Wright, was quite popular in her day but is rarely thought of today. www.Organic Jesus.com/a-voice-in-the-wilderness

The Man Who Was Thursday by G. K. Chesterton—The man whose theological writings had a deep impact on the conversion of C. S.

Lewis (and thousands, if not millions, of others) was also a great fiction writer. A thriller with hints of Christian allegory, this book is hard to put down. *The Napoleon of Notting Hill* is also a great read. www.OrganicJesus.com/the-man-who-was-thursday

Lilith by George MacDonald—J.R.R. Tolkien, C. S. Lewis, Madeleine L'Engle, W. H. Auden, and hundreds of other writers all credit the fantasies of MacDonald as greatly impacting their own work. *Lilith* is one of MacDonald's final books and also one of his deepest. www.OrganicJesus.com/lilith

Honorable Mentions from the Files of Free

Ben-Hur by Lew Wallace. www.OrganicJesus.com/ben-hur

The Waste Land (poem) by T. S. Eliot. www.OrganicJesus.com/the-waste-land

The Minister's Black Veil (short story) by Nathaniel Hawthorne. www.OrganicJesus.com/the-ministers-black-veil

The Death of Ivan Ilyich (novella) by Leo Tolstoy. www.OrganicJesus.com/the-death-of-ivan-ilyich

Getting Social

Twitter: Tweet your top three favorite Christian fiction titles: #ChristianLit.

Pinterest: Create a board called "Christian Fiction" full of all your favorite books with Christian themes.

Instagram: Go to a library book sale and find a Christian book you have never read. Take a picture of the book. If you've never been to a library book sale, you are missing out! You can usually grab an entire bag of books for a buck: #ChristianLit.

LinkedIn: Add "Speed-Reader" as a job skill. Now try to speed-read the next chapter of this book in one minute and see what you come away with.

Facebook: Post your five favorite Christian books and ask your friends and family to give their recommendations.

WhichBibleHero AreYou?

What are you most likely to do in the shower?

- A. Sing (+1)
- B. Wash-rinse-wash-done (+3)
- C. Make it hot but not too hot (+5)
- D. Organize the soap bottles in alphabetical order (+7)
- E. Leave on my underwear because nobody (not even me) should have to see me naked (+9)
- F. Make it steamy (+11)

Chapter Five

History of the World, Part 2

#ReligiouslyNonreligious

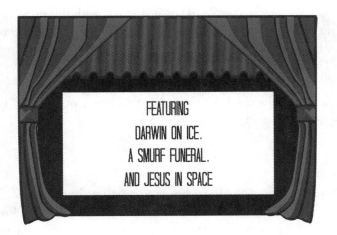

FEATURING
DARWIN ON ICE.
A SMURF FUNERAL.
AND JESUS IN SPACE

The Buddhist monk (he was a full-on monk—orange robe, shaved head, peaceful disposition), despite his peaceful nature, grabbed my hand harshly and told me to come with him. His hand was softer than I expected, and two things immediately popped into my head:

1. Was holding hands really necessary?

   2. Did he use moisturizer? Because this was seriously like hold-
      ing a newborn.

I had gotten acquainted with the monk over the past several
weeks in a college course in Judaism. He became the first person of
Eastern religious faith I had ever gotten to know and the first man I
had ever held hands with. He had petitioned the course at the start
of the quarter and was now considering taking more, which is why
he took my hand and asked me to lead him to the administration
offices.

As I walked across the quad holding hands with this grown, well-
moisturized monk, I realized I had come a long way since graduat-
ing high school. As a comparative religion major at a non-Christian
school, I had met a lot of people of different faiths, from Wiccans
to Hare Krishnas. When your faith is strong and your heart is open
to it, studying the wackiness of other religions can help you better
understand the wackiness of your own.

There are more than four thousand religions in the world. They
range from profound to outright crazy and even deadly. With so
many religions, no wonder so many people cannot decide what they
believe. If you were to spend a serious amount of time studying each
of them, chances are you would die before you were finished.

So it's fair to ask, how can you ever really know you believe in
the right one? Should you just go with the most popular one and
hope for the best?

If Christianity is the one true way and you do not believe in
Christianity because you've never heard of it, then do you go to hell
because you never had the chance to hear what it was about?

This book isn't about why other religions are wrong. It's not
even about why Christianity is right. This book is about reexplor-
ing the Christianity that even Christians have forgotten. One of the
greatest things God has shown me is that if you want your faith to

be strong—if you really want a relationship with God—then you have to believe because you know the other options. You have to let God reveal himself to *you* firsthand, and not to other people who tell you about him. Other people might get you started on your path to faith, but a strong foundation of belief can only happen when you come to the conclusion on your own.

It's a somewhat popular notion that Christians believe in Christianity, and our goal is to get others to believe in it as well. I suppose that is Christianity's objective as a religion, but we're not called by Christ to be institutionalized in the walls of a church; we are called to tell the good news to the world. So the question for a Christian shouldn't be whether a person can be saved if he or she hasn't heard about Christ; the question should be, why is there a person who hasn't heard about Christ?

A friend of mine told me not long ago that he really wants to understand the Bible so he can be "prepared to give answers."

"Why?" I asked him.

"Because that's what we're supposed to do."

I shrugged. "Perhaps. But do you really think that any answer you give a person will convert them?"

"Why not?"

"So you believe you can convert someone through knowledge of the Bible?"

"Maybe. And doesn't the Bible say that we should be prepared to have an answer for the reason that we believe?"

I nodded. "But it doesn't say to have an answer from the Bible."

He was quiet.

"Look, I'm not saying you shouldn't read the Bible. I'm not saying you shouldn't have answers from the Bible. What I'm saying is that you probably won't convert someone by giving answers to difficult questions. People have spent two thousand years giving answers to difficult questions. There are theologically grounded answers to every question that people have had. And people still don't believe."

"So how do you make someone believe?"

"You don't. You can't make someone believe anything. But if

you really want to give an answer to the hope that you have—the belief that you have salvation through Jesus Christ—then you have to answer by your actions."

I paused. "You've heard actions speak louder than words?"

"Of course."

"That's how you answer. Let them see your actions in suffering, grief, joy, and peace. Let them see that in all things you turn to God. Because if you want someone to believe in God, you have to show them God, and the only way to show them God is through your actions."

In the course of my life, I have been actively a part of four churches, two that grew a lot and two that never really could take off. There are a lot of reasons for growth and a lot of reasons for lack thereof. But the similarity I saw in the two that grew is simple: they were mission based. They called their flock to be more than just believers; they called them to go into the world and help the needy, teach the gospel, and experience Christ—and curiously enough, they encouraged people to do all this not with words, but with actions.

WikiBreak

Christianity is kind of a cult. Acts 11:26 and Acts 26:28 were the first time anyone used the term *Christian*, but it was more in reference to a group of people who were Jewish but belonged to a sect or cult within Judaism. There were God-fearing, temple-going Jews who believed in Jesus Christ.

So when did Christianity become less Jewish and more its own religion? It certainly didn't happen overnight. Scholars have argued quite extensively about when it happened, but the thing is, there was no one moment. It was a progression of many moments.

One thing is certain, however: it might never have happened if not for a fiery little Jewish convert by the name of Saul of Tarsus, whom you probably know as the apostle Paul. There's evidence that the Pharisee Gamaliel and many other early Jewish leaders believed Jesus was the Messiah. But Paul was one of the first to question the old covenant and say that Gentiles didn't need to be circumcised to be saved—that salvation was through Christ alone, not through keeping Jewish religious laws.

It is this issue of circumcision, the poster child of those laws, that many might mark as the first moment of progression away from Judaism. In AD 50, the Council of Jerusalem decided that circumcision was not required for salvation.

As late as the first century, one hundred years after Christ was resurrected, there were communities of Jewish Christians. But the writings of a Roman political leader, Pliny the Younger, reveal that the Romans did not view Christians as Jewish because they were not paying the Jewish tax. This is one of the early evidences that a separation was happening. But it really wasn't until more than 150 years from its formation that Christianity began taking shape as an independent religion apart from Judaism.

A few years ago, a pastor told me, "I know I have to trust in God, and maybe this will always be a smaller church—but I really want it to grow, and I just don't know why it isn't."

"What kind of mission projects do you have going on?"

He shrugged. "I had a young man ask me to pray for him about possibly becoming a missionary a few months back."

"This is my observation, so take it for what it's worth, but in my experience, the churches that have really grown are the ones that encourage every person in the church to do mission trips—even if they're short ones. Mission trips change people."

He nodded in agreement as he looked at his watch. "I've read a lot about church growth. I've heard that before. But we're a small church—and we're not that kind of church."

It was as if he was so concerned with getting his church to grow that he failed to realize that the people needed to grow first.

On the opposite end of the spectrum are people who preach the gospel a little too aggressively or in a way that makes no difference to people. When I was in college, I worked at the college library. Every day a young man from Kenya would come to me and, with a bright, contagious smile that you couldn't help smile back at, he would say, "Sir, may I share the gospel with you?"

The first time, I was caught off guard and said yes to be polite. I figured he would read something like, "God so loved the world that he gave his only Son. . . ." But he didn't. He read Leviticus 14:6: "He is then to take the live bird and dip it, together with the cedar wood, the scarlet yarn and the hyssop, into the blood of the bird that was killed over the fresh water."

He sighed when he finished reading it and said, "Isn't God's love beautiful?"

I imagined that this was a trick question, but for the life of me, I couldn't figure out what the trick was, so I said, "Sure, why not."

He smiled and closed his Bible. "Thank you for letting me share God's love with you."

The next day he found me again and asked the same question. This time I was more prepared. I said, "I really have a lot to do and I don't want to get in trouble with my supervisor."

That dumb, contagious smile came out again, and he said, "Can you spare just a couple of seconds for God?"

Conviction overtook me. I feared that if I said no, God would send lightning and kill me on the spot. So I nodded and braced myself for another lesson from the Torah. This time, however, he decided it was time to get a little more modern by jumping into the New Testament. But instead of a nice parable or beatitude, he put it in high gear and switched to Revelation 21:13: "There were three gates on the east, three on the north, three on the south and three on the west."

He giggled when he finished and said, "Don't you agree?"

"Yep," I said going back to shelving as it became clearer that he was just opening up his Bible and randomly selecting passages.

"Sir, I would like to ask you if you'd like to know Jesus personally."

I was confused. He really thought he had saved me by throwing out a verse from Leviticus and Revelation. I wasn't really sure what to say, so I said, "I'm a Christian."

His big smile left. He was really hoping for a saving. He nodded and said, "I will continue to pray for your soul. I hope you will know Jesus personally one day."

Throughout the semester he would occasionally come to me and ask to share something, and he continued to be convinced that I didn't know Jesus personally, but I'm not sure why.

Checklist of a Cult

[SHARE]

With more than four thousand religions in the world, you should obviously ask yourself, am I in the right one? For safety's sake, you should also ask if you are in a cult. Below is a checklist to make sure you are not.

☐ They can't stop talking about what an amazing person you are—until you sign on the dotted line.

☐ Other churches are ridiculed and put down while their church is built up.

☐ They point out that while deeds don't get you into heaven, not doing them gets you into hell.

☐ When you ask what happened to another member who mysteriously is no longer around, you are told never to ask such things.

☐ Every time you ask about something the church is doing that is questionable (like elders taking little girls as brides), they say, "That's a very good question—but before I answer, let's go do something awesome." Then they quietly mumble, "And hope you forget that you asked."

☐ The beliefs of the leader are the only thing that matters.

☐ You are asked to give up all your belongings and assets in return for a robe and maybe sandals. And the robe isn't even nice; it stinks of BO.

☐ You are told to cut ties with family and friends because they're evil.

☐ Private time is now group time. You are encouraged never to be alone.

☐ Your leader tells you to ignore people who say you are in a cult (including that pesky news reporter who keeps asking why you are in a cult).

The strongest case for Christianity isn't in the words of believers, and it isn't in the debates between other religions. It is in actions. When we look at Christ and consider all that he did, his greatest teachings weren't so much in what he said but what he did. His greatest action was of course going to the cross, but his entire ministry was built on actions that serve as examples for believers.

When we go out into the world and we simply love people—when we help the needy, when our mission isn't to get wealth but to surrender or get rid of wealth—then I can only imagine what this world would look like. Unfortunately, many Christians are so focused on family, career, and their general livelihood that they can only devote, at best, one or two hours a week for God. When I read the Bible, I sometimes think about how the first Christians must have lived—what their churches looked like, what their leaders looked like, and what worship looked like. I doubt that much of it resembled what we've got today. It wasn't loud. The churches weren't big; they were homes, more or less. The leaders weren't fancy and the worship wasn't hip. There wasn't loud music with harmonizing vocals. There weren't lights to help make things more emotional. I don't imagine things were perfect—far from it. It was raw. But it worked.

A lot of Christians entered the religion program at the college I went to, and their mission was clear: they wanted to find proof that all the other religions were wrong. My own agenda was to hear what other religions said. To be a follower of Christ doesn't mean you have to switch on your Jesus button when a Buddhist sits next to you; to be a follower means that when a Buddhist sits down next to you, you love them like they are your own brother. You treat them kindly. You respect them.

The gospel comes alive when we live it, not when we memorize it so we can spout it off at a person who doesn't believe like us.

Throughout college I read about all the major religions, studied them, wrote essays on them, took tests on them. When I left, I was certain of one thing: they weren't completely wrong. But I walked away feeling stronger in faith; I had met the other religions and could honestly say that Christ is the way, the truth, and the life.

Other "Christian" students weren't so lucky.

During my first year, I met a woman who was returning to school because her children were older and she needed something to do. She was angry. For all her life, she had belonged to a rather conservative church. "They lied to me," she explained the first day I met her. "There are so many flaws within Christianity."

It was a common story. She hadn't been lied to, but it was easy to relate to her. Nobody but God is perfect—and no religion is perfect. But that's the way it's often portrayed. I don't believe I've ever heard a sermon on the flaws in Christianity. I've never heard of pastors preaching about the seeming inconsistencies in the Bible and how they can be explained because they aren't really inconsistencies at all.

I encountered the woman off and on throughout my time in college, and her story was always the same: they lied. The longer she was in the program, the more bitter she got. But instead of directing her anger toward the church, she directed it at God.

No one wants to admit the flaws of their child. That's what Christianity is: the "child" of imperfect humans responding to God's perfect redemption. The flaws are there; they're not hidden. But no one talks about them openly—so of course they must be really bad. Except they're not. The flaws don't discredit the mission of the church. They don't even change theology. I couldn't help but wonder what would have happened if the woman hadn't been "lied" to—if instead she'd found a safe place to ask questions and gotten satisfying answers. I imagine she would have been a stronger Christian.

A lot of Christians I talked to offered to pray for me as I continued my studies. They saw me as walking in a dangerous place. To many believers, it's fine to study other beliefs as long as you have an educated Christian holding your hand. It made me wonder how strong this whole Christianity thing was when you couldn't see what else was out there without the entire thing collapsing. I knew that God was stronger than any teaching out there, and if that was true, then he'd hold up against all things.

USELESS POLL

Other religions . . .

A. scare me.
B. should be condemned, shamed, and destroyed.
C. should be respected.
D. are all true.

To be part of this poll, visit:
www.OrganicJesus.com/useless-polls

The danger of studying other religions only exists when you have been raised with a set of values that guards you from the realities of the world. So many kids lose their way in college not because of the environment, but because they weren't prepared for the environment.

There is a degree of truth in all religions, and God works everything to his will, so even though I personally believe salvation is found only in Christ, I know that I can find glimpses of God in most other religions.

When I was working on my degree, a Bible student said, "I get that you want to know about other religions so you can defend your faith, but why not do it at a Christian school?" The answer for me was simple: "Because I want to learn from someone who's not trying to disprove other religions." I was never trying to disprove anything; I only wanted to have a better understanding.

Match the Religion

Draw lines to match the religion with the description. Pat yourself on the back if the line is straight.[1] *(See page 224 for answer key.)*

Judaism	Monotheistic religion that began in the fifteenth century. It teaches the equality of all and believes we should have oneness with God. Prayer is an important part of spiritual life and helps connect you with God.
Islam	Polytheistic religion believed to have begun in 1400 BC. Its principal beliefs are found in a set of texts known as the Vedas. You create your own destiny based on your actions.
Hinduism	Monotheistic religion that began in the seventh century. Followers seek to keep the five pillars (confession of faith, prayer, alms [giving money to needy causes], fasting, and pilgrimage). You must submit to God. There will be a resurrection of the dead, and people will go to either paradise or hell.
Buddhism	Monotheistic religion that began in the 1800s in the Middle East. Its name means "The Glory of God." Believes that God sends messengers to reveal himself to humans, and that all humanity and all religions are united under one God.
Shintoism	Monotheistic religion founded in the nineteenth century. Promotes the "Joyous Life," which can come from acts of charity. Believes that the body is only borrowed.
Sikhism	Pantheistic religion that began in 600 BC. It teaches nonviolence and believes that all people have a soul, which creates its own destiny. We should learn to control our mind, because our mind can bring us away from our soul. The ultimate goal is liberation of the soul.
Baháʾí	Monotheistic religion believed to be founded during the Bronze Age. Follows thirteen principles of faith. Believes that we need to sanctify our life to have a closer relationship with God.
Jainism	Began in the 1900s. Followers believe that its prophets were destined to save mankind from suffering. Believes in aiding the poor over building fancy shrines; religious ceremonies should be simple and modest, because money is better spent helping the poor.
Hòa Hảo	Polytheistic religion that literally means "the way of gods." Believes that spirits live in all natural places. Prior to World War II, it was the main religion of Japan.
Tenriism	One of the few religions that does not say whether there is or isn't a supreme being. Teaches that bad actions bring bad consequences and, similarly, good actions bring good consequences. The ultimate goal is to reach a state where you free yourself of suffering, which happens by getting rid of greed, hatred, and ignorance.

---

1. Drawing in this book means you cannot list it as "collectible" when you sell it used to someone else.

Now let's really have fun. In three sentences or less, use the space below to write what Christianity teaches:

_____

_____

_____

On the other end of the spectrum, people would say, "You've read about all the religions. How can you still believe there is only one true religion?" Again the answer is easy: because there's absolute harmony in Christianity. It all comes together and works—it makes sense. When I hear people angry with Christianity, it's as if they're blinded by pride, fogged by what some Christian did to them.

In the end, there really was no other religion so beautifully and perfectly put together. It's unfortunate that for two thousand years, people have been distorting it and turning it into something it is not.

Getting Social

Twitter: Think about any religion besides Christianity and tweet how you can see God's presence in it: #GodLovesAll.

Pinterest: Create a board called "A World of Religions" full of information about different religions around the world.

Instagram: Take a picture of a synagogue, mosque, or temple: #GodLovesAll.

LinkedIn: Become friends with a rabbi. Endorse all his job skills.

Facebook: Post about any religion besides Christianity. Talk about how you can see God's presence in it.

Which Bible Hero Are You?

What music would you most likely be caught listening to?

- A. Folk music (+1)
- B. Classical all the way (+3)
- C. What my parents listened to (+5)
- D. Self-help audio books (+7)
- E. Rap and hip-hop (+9)
- F. Heavy metal (+11)

Chapter Six

East of Eden

#ChristianFlatulence

SHARE

There is no greater advocate for satan[1] than some Christians. Ask a person why he or she doesn't believe and there is a good chance you'll hear something about a Christian who wronged that person. Maybe it won't be the only reason, but it will be a reason.

Several years ago, I was minding my own business in a library when a deceptively normal-looking man sat next to me and began talking to me about the world and all its flaws. Notably, he zeroed in on what we should do about the Muslim problem. "In World

---

1. Note to members of the grammar police: I realize *satan* is supposed to be uppercased, but I've never wanted to give him that kind of respect.

War II, we rounded up all the Asians and Chinese[2] and put them in camps. That's what we should do with Muslims. Problem solved."

"What problem does that solve exactly?"

He looked at me like I was the dumbest person he had ever met. "The terrorism problem."

"How many terrorist attacks have been committed by Muslims living in America?"

He thought for a moment. I could tell he thought this question was a trick—as if he really wanted to say "9/11" but knew I'd twist his words around by saying something ridiculous, like 9/11 *wasn't* an attack by American Muslims.[3] After scratching his chin in an attempt to muster profound wisdom, he explained, "There was the one in San Bernardino." Seconds later, he added, "It's not about how many they have committed; it's about how many they will commit."

"Future-proofing America, then?"

"Exactly."

"Why stop at Muslims? Why not the Jews? Didn't they kill Jesus?"

"If the government would allow it, why not?"

"You think they'd allow it? The government?"

"Not with the liberals in office." He paused and then added, angrily, "I'm the minority now. My rights are being violated, and that's just wrong. My people founded this nation. I'm a Christian."

"Of course you are."

Most people have probably had conversations that went down like this. Maybe not as extreme—or maybe more extreme. They give rise to this question: If Christianity is so great that the very Spirit of God indwells believers, then why are so many Christians so flawed?

There's a popular slogan: "I'm not perfect. I'm just saved." It's what many Christians use to excuse their unrighteous behavior. Under this theory, Christians can essentially do anything and then shrug their shoulders and say, "I'm not perfect. I'm just saved." It's

---

2. Yes, this man really didn't know that Chinese were Asian or that the internment camps he was mentioning were actually for Japanese Americans, not Asians.

3. Or Muslims of any sort, for that matter.

like the ultimate "Get Out of Jail Free" card. Why would Christians even want to be more than just okay? If they can live the life they want to live and just keep using the card, then the religion starts to feel a little . . . cheap.

It's true that some Christians have tried to find a theology of salvation by deeds as a way of ensuring we live more Christian lives. It never works, of course, because if we could save ourselves by works then there would be no point in a Redeemer. We are saved by grace. But because of grace we should be moved by the Spirit to do good deeds, which is how we begin to have a relationship with God and experience his presence.

The problem isn't that the theology is flawed or even wrong; the problem is that many Christians would rather just not accept the grace of God. They want heaven—who doesn't?—but they don't want to grow closer to God; they don't want to experience God. Does that mean that if you aren't doing good deeds—if you aren't experiencing God by putting grace in motion through your actions —then you aren't really a Christian? More realistically, it means that you aren't a mature Christian. God wants us to relate to him, but he is not going to force us to do so.

There are a lot of motivated Christians who truly are experiencing God through the way they live. But they're not the ones who get attention. Nobody wants to see a reality show about a nice person who lives a righteous life; they want to see someone who makes a spectacle of things.

They don't want to hear someone tell them how to experience God; they want to hear someone tell them what they want to hear— live their sinful life; God forgives them. They can be rich. They can have earthly happiness.

I'm always a little shocked by the ads on Christian radio. They're about either getting rich, or having some sort of cosmetic surgery to make us more heavenly looking, or getting out of debt. The focus isn't a relationship with God; it's on having a relationship with ourselves.

If you really want to understand Christianity, you can't look to see who all the sinners are. And so we turn to the saints.

In 1517, a young Catholic priest by the name of Martin Luther famously posted his Ninety-Five Theses on the door of the church in Wittenberg, Germany. That act set religion on fire, and it forever cemented Luther's name as the founder of one of the largest Christian movements in Christianity. Luther translated the Bible, wrote hymns, and wrote volumes on theology. What's not to love about the guy? If he hadn't been so darn Lutheran, the Catholic Church probably would have sainted him.

USELESS POLL

My favorite church schism is . . .

A. the Schism of Marcionism (AD 150).
B. the Oriental Orthodox Schism (AD 451).
C. the East-West Schism of 1054 (AD 1054).
D. the Protestant Reformation (AD 1517).

To be part of this poll, visit:
www.OrganicJesus.com/useless-polls

Surely we can model our life after good old Luther, right? Surely we can look at him and say, "See! Christians are good!" Surely! But Lutherans had a dirty little secret—a very open one at that, no secret at all: Martin Luther, the great church reformer, hated Jews. Like, *really* hated them. Like, wrote entire books on the subject.

In 1536, with the support of Luther, a mandate was issued that prohibited Jews in Saxony, Brandenburg, and Silesia from doing business. In one of his most famous books on the subject, *On the Jews and Their Lies*, Luther believed the Jewish people were outright evil and their schools, synagogues, and prayer books should all be burned. In his second-to-last sermon before his death, Luther said we should treat Jews a little more Christianly. Finally old Luther had relented, right? Um . . . no. He opened his mouth again and explained what he meant. We should tell the Jews that if they don't convert to Christianity, then we would have to banish them from the land and not permit them to live around us. But if they convert, then we should of course be kind to them—because that's the Christian way: love your enemies, whereby they convert to your ways and hence are no longer your enemies.

Okay, but that's just a fluke. John Calvin was one of the good ol'

boys of the Protestant Reformation[4] and one of the greatest thinkers of the Christian faith. Unlike Luther, Calvin's views on Jews are
more a matter of debate. He agreed that Jews were wrong about
their belief, but he never went as far as writing books about them
being banished. So Calvin's surely a person we can look to when we
want a good Christian role model, right?

Well . . . there *is* the whole Michael Servetus thing.[5] Calvin sort
of helped plan his execution. Whoops.

Okay, then, there are always the popes, right?

Really? The list of papal flaws could take up entire books. Some
of the greater misses of the popes include, but aren't limited to, the
following:

- According to popular legend, Popes John VII and John XII
  both died while engaging in sexual misconduct.
- Pope Benedict IX was offered money to resign as pope. He
  took it but then felt bad, though not about the taking-money
  thing—about giving up his position. He ended up being elected
  pope not once, not twice, but three times.
- Pope Sergius III, like many other popes, had a bad reputation
  for ordering the deaths of his rivals. But his seed of evil didn't
  stop there—literally. He fathered an illegitimate child who
  later also became a pope.
- Pope Stephen VI had his predecessor (Pope Formosus) dug up
  from his grave and put on trial.[6] The old, smelly pope (Formosus,
  not Stephen—although some suspect Stephen did have smelly
  feet) was propped up on a throne and actually asked questions.
  Unfortunately, Formosus couldn't answer the questions, being
  dead, so a deacon answered on his behalf. And here's where
  it gets weird (that last part was only gruesome): they actually

---

4. So humble that he didn't even get a religion named after him like his contemporary, Martin Luther.
5. A now-forgotten theologian who was deemed a heretic by both Protestants
   and Catholics.
6. I kid you not—he had a corpse put on trial.

found the smelly pope guilty and cut off his fingers. Formosus was then reinterred and his papacy was annulled.

Here's the thing: if you really want to understand Christianity, you can't look to see who all the sinners are, and you can't look to see who all the saints are. You can only look at who Jesus Christ is. When we look at the church for answers, we see those who have fallen; when we look at God, we see the relationship he wants to have with us.

What I frequently hear from fallen Christians is how strict their parents were, what their church did to their family, or who rubbed them the wrong way. I never hear a person say, "I no longer believe because God's a real jerk." God doesn't turn people away; people do.

Mark Twain famously said that if we want to save the world, then we should bring home all the missionaries and have them convert the Christians. Twain was a bitter, sad man, but he had very wise things to say about Christianity. Pastors often talk a lot about spiritual revival, but for that to take place, Christians themselves need to be revived. They need to wake up to what they used to believe. They need to experience God once more. Maybe next time you think about converting your non-Christian neighbor, you should consider converting the Christian one as well.

SHARE How to Convert Anyone to Christianity

1. Pray.

2. Go to your closet. Find something that says "I'm a normal person";[7] jeans with holes around one (but not both) of the knees are not only acceptable, but encouraged.

3. Invite the person to an event where they would never guess you are about to talk to them about Jesus. They cannot, under any circumstances, know that you are going to have "The Talk" with

---

7. Make sure the sock color matches the belt color.

them—otherwise they might feel like they are being tricked. One way to ask them is to suggest you need advice or perhaps that you need help with your schoolwork. Remember to pick a setting that makes it difficult for them to make a scene.

4. Arrive at the meeting place a little late and emphasize the privilege it is for them to be around you. Make them feel special that you have chosen them to help you.

5. Begin your conversation by talking about worldly things. Make them understand that you are a normal person. Talk about fine beers, PG-13 movies, and hip-hop music. Encourage them to also tell you their favorite things.

6. Interrupt them to tell them you didn't always like such fine things, but then you met a man named Jesus. They will probably make a joke about this and say they also know a man named Jesus and he mows their lawn. Use this point to belittle them and make them feel like a racist.

7. Begin telling them about all the amazing things that have happened in your life since becoming a Christian. Emphasize that all the things you used to do you still do, but now they are more Christian. Make believing seem worldly. Talk about the zombie cosplay club you belong to that's just for Christians. Mention how you are now wealthier, you are growing back hair that you had previously lost, and you no longer have to wear deodorant because you no longer have any sort of body odor.

8. There will be awkward and uncomfortable silence at this point. The person has already begun looking for an excuse to leave. They've looked at their watch several times and have even mentioned needing to leave. It's important at this point that you place your hand on top of their wrist and hold it against the table. This will show you aren't letting them leave just yet. It will

make them feel threatened and they will begin to see who's in charge. Ask them if they'd like to give their life to Jesus; make your grip tighter as you ask this.

9. They will still be in denial at this point. Tell them that you'd like to pray for them and before they can say no, start praying. Pray loudly and passionately. Don't worry about all the people who can hear you—pray as loudly as possible about all the things your friend has done to sin; if you can cry, you should cry. When you're finished, attempt to hug them. They might be so overwhelmed by your prayer they could reject the hug. Don't take offense—they have heard what you have said and it has changed their opinion of you.

10. Before they leave, remind them of two things: (1) your church meets Sundays at 10:00 a.m., and (2) they agreed to pay for your meal. Pat yourself on the back, brave Christian—you have changed the heart and mind of an unsaved person!

11. When your attempt fails, then rethink your strategy; consider approaching the person as a follower of Christ and not as a person just trying to score a few church points with hurtful tricks. Remember that you are an instrument of God—God wants to use you to show his love to those who don't know his love. Explaining the love of God will never be as powerful as showing the love of God through actions.

When I was young, I asked a relative why he didn't go to church. He answered, "Because I don't like being preached to." The comment has always stuck with me. Why would anyone want to be preached to? Is the church's role to make you feel like a sinner? To guilt you into believing?

Salvation: it's a life-altering thing, but it takes a certain amount of discipline. When you first believe, your life is new and refreshed. But too often, the moment of salvation is so heavily emphasized that it's hard to preserve that feeling when life catches up. Yet a lot of churches think it's their role to help you keep that first edge no matter what life throws at you.

Sometimes I picture the following scene: A preacher is trying his hardest to get people excited. Finally, after doing everything he knows how to get them to listen, he says the one thing that can wake up pretty much anyone: "Jesus farted."

You won't find that passage in any translation of the Bible I know of, but the pastor starts to make a convincing case that archaeological evidence supports the claim. The disciples, he continues, also farted. So did Mary and Joseph and a bunch of other people in the Bible. There was a whole lot of farting going on—or, as the pastor says so eloquently, "Fart, fart, *fart*." He says the last one particularly loudly and follows with his best imitation of what a biblical fart sounds like. (In case you are wondering, biblical farts sound very similar to modern farts.)

The pastor is not trying to preach a sermon on the flatulence of the Messiah. Actually, he's talking about tithing, a topic that can easily silence a room. But when, midway through the sermon, he describes a meal Jesus and the disciples had before going to the synagogue, and how that meal almost certainly caused a few toots, well . . . everyone immediately perks up at the mention of the immaculate fart. The silence of the congregation, who fear a lecture on not giving enough money, turns to a riot of laugher. Women are in tears. One large man punctuates his laughter by stomping his feet and clapping his hands. An older woman has to fan herself. A teenager makes a farting sound, and several others join her. Worst of all is a small child two rows back who says, "Mommy, I peed." The sermon might as well have been titled "The Fart Heard Around the World."

It's not that I don't like a good fart joke—I do. But in the context of a sermon, the joke feels . . . cheap. Unfortunately, cheap is what some pastors have resorted to, and so too a lot of churchgoing Christians. Fewer and fewer want pastors who know Hebrew and have a degree in biblical hermeneutics; more and more want entertainers who can reference both *South Park* and the Bible in the same sentence.

Churches may be run as nonprofits, but they're still a business.

And pastors have to fill seats every Sunday if they are going to stay in business. For some, that means taking a cue from Adam Sandler. But at what cost? Sometimes the holy feels lost.

WikiBreak

Farting, or flatulence, is nothing to be embarrassed about. It happens to the best of us. Gas, for the most part, is really nothing more than a bunch of bacterial fermentation in your colon.

Surprisingly, farts do have some religious origins—not biblical, mind you, but religious nonetheless. In the fifth century, the great (and sainted) theologian Augustine wrote what is considered one of the great books of Christian theology: *The City of God*. Among the splendid insights Augustine offered, he said that there were men who "have such command of their bowels, that they can break wind continuously at will, so as to produce the effect of singing" (14.24). Yes, Augustine—a man whom the Catholic Church canonized; who is studied at the most prestigious universities of the world; who may just be one of the greatest Christian thinkers who ever lived—said that men could basically sing songs with their farts.

Christianity is rooted in the premise that we are a deeply flawed people who need to be saved. The problem is, people are so obsessed with the flaws of the religion that they fail to see the truth of the God-man.

The New Testament frequently talks about grace and mercy. They're very poetic-sounding words whose meaning is sometimes lost. *Grace* is getting what you don't deserve; *mercy* is not getting what you do deserve. The emphasis of church never needs to be about what we're doing; it should be on the reward.

Christianity is not without its flaws, but there is reward in its message—not the message of its people but the message of its founder, Jesus Christ. Sometimes we are so eager to hide the flaws that we make Christianity sound exciting and even funny. We tell a fart joke here and there. We've told so many, that belief in Christianity almost seems like a joke in itself.

There's nothing wrong with a little entertainment, with enjoying and even having fun with what you believe. But the emphasis has to be on the reward: on grace and on mercy—on the relationship with God.

Getting Social

Twitter: Tweet what grace and mercy mean to you: #aliveinChrist.

Pinterest: Create a board called "Christian Sinners" full of all your favorite fallen saints.

Instagram: Take a picture of someone performing a random act of kindness: #grace.

LinkedIn: Search LinkedIn for a nonprofit group you could volunteer at. Now go outside your comfort zone and volunteer.

Facebook: Post what *grace* and *mercy* mean to you.

WhichBibleHero AreYou?

What is your preferred role at church?

A. Praise team (+1)

B. Comfort ministry (+3)

C. Behind the scenes and not getting acknowledged (+5)

D. Pastor (+7)

E. Person who does the announcements (+9)

F. Youth ministry (+11)

ChapterSeven

Can You Put That Miracle in the Form of a Pill?

#RXJesus

Happy Pill   **Poison Pill**   **Jesus Pill**

Miracles. They make us feel all warm and fuzzy. Peter fled Rome to avoid execution, but along the way he received a vision of Jesus, who was also traveling. When Peter asked him where he was going, Jesus said he was heading to Rome to be crucified again. Peter took this miraculous vision as a sign that he should return as well. When he arrived, he asked to be crucified upside down on a cross.

What a delightful, inspirational story! Except for one thing: there's very little truth to it. Sure, it's possible that Peter was crucified upside down. And it's also possible that I'll wake up tomorrow transformed into a toad.

Here's the problem. Instead of considering the historical integrity of the story, we pass it around among believers for motivation. In Peter's case, the legend was most likely created to help Christians feel better about their own struggles.

That's all well and good, but such legends have an unfortunate effect once they're revealed as mere tall tales: they discredit the truth. People think, "If this is made up, then that's probably made up too." If early Christians were telling little white lies about Peter, then it makes sense that they were also lying about Christ himself.

When it came to miracles, Jesus was the man. He was healing here, walking on water there, feeding thousands with a single loaf of bread, turning water into wine. He kind of sounds like a super-hero. But how many miracles were actually recorded? The way people talk you'd think there were hundreds, thousands even. There weren't. The number is actually much lower.

It's thirty-seven.[1]

That's not a small number; it's certainly more miracles than I've performed.[2] But for Christ? He could do anything, and yet thirty-seven was the best he could come up with? Numerologists can't even do much with that number.

Did he do more miracles than are recorded? Absolutely.[3] But—and it's a big but—they are left out of the Scriptures. There's plenty in the Bible to suggest that people expected Jesus to do miracles, which implies that he did a lot of them. In John 2:1, before Jesus had even begun his public ministry, his mother asked him to turn water into wine. She knew Jesus could do it because moms don't just ask their kids to perform miracles unless they can actually do

---

1. This is the conservative answer. It really depends on what you consider a miracle. For the sake of this book, a recorded miracle is a single miracle—so, for example, in one miracle Jesus fed 4,000 people. Some people will count different things as miracles, and the number gets a little higher.
2. If you are wondering, there was that one time I got my cat in her carrier without a single scratch, but this may also be considered luck.
3. John 21:25 says that not everything Jesus did is recorded because that would fill more than a few books.

them, which meant he had probably done lots and lots of miracles growing up.[4]

Do miracles happen? Of course. But we can't rest our faith on miracles. We can't wait for miracles to come our way before we believe.

The skeptic in all of us has a tendency to look at things and discredit them. But miracles do happen.

In 1968, a Muslim mechanic in Egypt looked across the street at Saint Mary's Church and saw something quite . . . miraculous: an apparition of Mary. Yes—crazy man sees crazy thing; just another day, right? Not so much. The apparition continued to appear off and on for about three years. Hundreds flocked to the church and witnessed the sight, and not just crazy Christians. Jews saw it. Other Muslims saw it. Atheists saw it. There are photos of the event.[5]

So what happened? What do scientists say of the event? Not a whole lot. There are a few theories, but they are just as bizarre as the miracle itself. Most scientists feel more comfortable tucking it away as something that simply cannot be explained.

In the Catholic and Eastern Orthodox churches, there's a little

USELESS POLL

When I think of miracles, I think . . .

A. I've been the "victim" of many miracles.

B. I believe in them, but I've never had one happen to me.

C. they happen all the time, but most people are too busy to notice.

D. it's a miracle I get up every morning!

E. I believe in them and I've experienced them.

To be part of this poll, visit: www.OrganicJesus.com/useless-polls

---

4. I like to imagine it looked a little like Oprah giving out cars. But instead of Oprah saying, "You get a car! And you get a car! And you get a car!" it was Jesus saying, "You get a miracle! And you get a miracle! And you get a miracle!"

5. Look up "Our Lady of Zeitoun" if you'd like to read more.

doctrine called incorruptibility. Basically, when we die, we decay and eventually become dust; without any of our bodily organs working, there's simply nothing there to keep our flesh alive. If we are embalmed, the process is slowed down. But everyone decays. Well, not everyone—and that's where the theory of incorruptibility comes into play. A few hundred years ago, both the Eastern Orthodox and Catholic churches began to record cases where righteous people died and their bodies remained in a non-decayed, lifelike state. Not only that, but it also was reported that they smelled divine and let out a floral scent.[6] It would be easy to say some embalming trick was used, but this is again an area where science cannot give an answer. And it's not a case where it happened to one person in a centralized area; there are dozens, if not hundreds, of such bodies. Visit Europe long enough and you are bound to stumble into a church that has one.

The thing about both of these miracles is this: What do they really teach us about faith? Entire books have been written about miracles; how do you feel after reading about these two? Do they make you want to live a better life? Do you want to believe if you don't already?

Probably not. More than likely you, like me, are thinking, "Well, that's certainly weird."

The miracles don't teach us anything. We aren't able to say, "That gives me deeper spiritual maturity, and now I feel closer to God."

Doubting Thomas gave one of the best examples of how God feels about miracles. Thomas missed his chance to see the risen Christ and then famously said that unless he put his fingers through the nail marks in Jesus's hands, he would not believe. When Christ met up with Thomas, he invited Thomas to follow through with his request. But he also told Thomas that those who have not seen but still believed were blessed (John 20:24–29).

There's nothing wrong with miracles. God can be kind of showy—but it doesn't have anything to do with faith. God doesn't

---

6. This is called "odour of sanctity."

want us to believe in a magician. He wants us to believe in a father figure—a person we can have a relationship with.

Curiously, the miracles that impact us most are the ones we do not often notice—the little things that happen which can only be explained as unexplainable. Not things that would make people say *Wow!*—just things that protect us and keep us close to God.

Have you ever paused and thought about all the little coincidences in your life that make your life what it is? Stopped to consider where you are and how you got there? I can think of hundreds, if not thousands, of ways my life would look different if just one small thing had been changed. They're coincidences—but they add up. Random occurrences, like strangers who said things that strangers do not normally say, leading to trips to the doctor and the discovery of medical conditions.

When you start adding up these coincidences, you start seeing that one of the greatest miracles is the way that God does work in your life—the way God puts the right person in the right place at the right time. You have no idea how many people *you* have affected without your even knowing it.

The funny thing is, these coincidences aren't reserved for believers only. A lot of Christians wrongly assume that believing in Jesus Christ gives them an insurance card that is just for them. It does give them salvation. But—brace yourself—God loves and cares for Muslims, Buddhists, atheists . . . he cares for all of us.

There isn't a dark cloud above a person who doesn't believe. Why don't bad things happen to nonbelievers? Why should they? Those who believe and those who don't believe are separated in one key way: salvation. God never leaves these people; he wants them to return to him. When they don't believe, they open themselves up to darkness and spiritual attacks. But God does not abandon them.

When we believe, we receive the ultimate gift from God: grace. And grace leads to blessings. We are blessed abundantly. Not with wealth and material things, but with spiritual things.

WikiBreak

Dropped Chalk. It's the kind of story to put chills down your spine. It has all the ingredients of a heartwarming Christian movie: an enraged college professor, a rebellious and passionate Christian with a heart of gold, and, of course, chalk.

As the story goes, the professor tells students that if there is a God, then he would prevent the chalk in his hand from breaking in two when it hit the floor. And so it goes that the chalk fell from the professor's hand, rolled off his pants, and dropped to the floor—unbroken.

It's a touching, warm, and certainly fuzzy story. Is that a tear in your eye right now?

The story isn't true, but people keep sending it and others keep falling for it. If you have email and a grandma, then I'm sure the story has been delivered to your inbox on multiple occasions.

The first time I got the email, I was in college and it came from an elderly woman. It was sent to me and about five hundred of her closest friends. The professor in the story taught at the University of Irvine. A few months later, I got the same email from the same person, but the professor's name and school had been changed. Over the years, I've seen dozens of variations, all naming different colleges and even different classes. Sometimes the teacher teaches math and other times science.

Variants of the story have been reported from way back in the pre-Internet days of the 1960s, but the Internet gave way to a brand-new kind of urban legend that spreads like a weed.

So if Jesus was doing all these miracles, then why aren't they documented? Very simply, the Gospels are a record of Jesus's teachings. So when it's recording a miracle, it's because Jesus was teaching through the miracle. Let's look at a few miracles of Jesus.[7]

---

7. Jesus's miracles can be easily broken down into four groups: healing, exorcism, resurrection, and control over nature.

Aside from rising from the dead, one of the miracles for which Jesus is most often remembered is walking on water. That's a pretty cool miracle. I can't walk on water, and I don't know anyone who can. But aside from the cool factor, what does walking on water teach us . . . or the disciples, for that matter? Of all the miracles that could have been documented, why that one?

It actually gives us a few points to think about. First, not to get all cheesy here, but this miracle happened on a dark and stormy night. The storm wasn't just bad, it was violent. What does that mean? Jesus is telling us that he comes when the season in our life is not good—that when times are bad, we are not alone.

Second, the disciples didn't know Jesus when they saw him! Have you ever wondered why the disciples are always failing to recognize the guy they've been palling around with for years? The same thing happened at the resurrection. I think two things are happening. One, disbelief: they don't believe it's him because what they are seeing can't be happening. Two, they are seeing the divine side of the human Jesus. This happens at a pivotal moment in the gospel of Matthew. Matthew 8:27 says, "And the men marveled, saying, 'What sort of man is this, that even winds and sea obey him?'" (ESV). In other words, Jesus is doing this to show them his authority.

Jesus also does several healing miracles. Let's look at one—the healing of a paralytic.[8] When I think of the term "healing miracle," what comes to mind is some crazy preacher knocking over a paralyzed person and shouting hysterically, "Walk!" What separates Jesus from a TV miracle worker is that he doesn't say "Walk!" And again, he's using a miracle to teach.

The first thing we should be aware of in this story is how the man gets to Jesus. His friends are literally carrying him. There's no real reason to show this—unless there *is* a reason! And if all three of the synoptic Gospels record it, then there is. The writers wanted to

---

8. Matthew 9:1–8; Mark 2:1–12; Luke 5:17–26.

show that these men cared deeply for their friend. Miracles happen all the time, but you really start seeing God's glory when friends shower you with love and support.

The friends don't stop at just getting the paralytic to where Jesus is teaching; when they see there's no possible way to get him to where Jesus is, they don't give up—they find a way! In this case, they lower the man from a roof.

Jesus sees their faith but does something unexpected. Instead of saying, "Walk!" he says, "Your sins are forgiven."

I imagine the man's heart was racing a million miles a minute as Jesus came to him. The moment he'd waited for his entire life had arrived—he would walk! But instead, Jesus simply tells him his sins are forgiven.

It doesn't say if the man was disappointed. I imagine he was more confused.

Jesus heals him moments later, but again, there's an important lesson to be learned: man cares about physical things, but God cares about spiritual things.

When Jesus saw this man, he didn't see a handicapped man—he saw a person who needed salvation. He didn't see what the man wanted but what he needed. We come to God all the time with our wants, but God responds to our needs instead.

Again the writers record this miracle to show Jesus's authority. Nobody but God can forgive sins. I can tell someone that I personally forgive him for wronging me, but only God can say that he is spiritually forgiven.

Finally, one of the most frequently cited miracles is the raising of Lazarus.[9] Like the other miracles, Jesus is revealing his authority, but there is so much more than that going on.

First, why did Jesus even bother going to Lazarus? He'd been known to phone it in,[10] and besides, as his disciples warned him, Lazarus lived in a dangerous place where people had it in for Jesus.

---

9. John 11:1–45.
10. See Matthew 8:5–13; Luke 7:1–10; John 4:46–54.

Going there posed a great risk; in fact, it is right after the miracle that the plot to kill Jesus begins.

Second, people often go to this story to point out the shortest verse in the Bible: "Jesus wept" (John 11:35). That's a funny thing to do considering that Lazarus is not going to stay dead. So why does Jesus weep? The gospel account doesn't say; most likely it's because Lazarus's friends are hurting. The statement shows the compassionate side of Jesus—when we hurt, he hurts. The fact that he can perform a miracle does not give him comfort. He loves us so much that he does not want us to suffer, and it deeply pains him when we do.

Third, why does Jesus wait four days? It's a powerful lesson in patience. Today more than ever, we want an immediate fix. We are Generation NOW. But man and God work differently. We cry out to God and say, "Fix this problem," and we are disappointed when it doesn't happen the moment our lips say "Amen." In this case, Jesus's followers assume wrongly that their prayer is not answered because Lazarus does not get better. But the point is that even when things seem hopeless and our prayers aren't answered, we should never give up hope. When Jesus said God would come through in John 11:4, that's exactly what he meant. When all hope was lost, God came through. He always does.

Finally, further down in verse 43, Jesus tells Lazarus to come out of the tomb. What is curious about this is that Jesus uses Lazarus's name. Why? One likely reason is because Jesus had a personal relationship with Lazarus. But the greater answer most likely points to the ultimate message of the miracle: we must be born again. The raising of Lazarus foreshadows the resurrection of Jesus Christ himself, and believing in his resurrection is where our own new life begins. That's why Jesus's calling Lazarus by his name is important: because the resurrection isn't a church thing, it's a personal thing. Jesus knows us each by name, and through the resurrection we aren't just raised to start a new life—we are raised to start a personal relationship with Christ.

There were quack preachers in Jesus's day just as there are today—people running around healing and attempting to do miraculous things. The gospel writers knew this. They knew that people were always looking for a person doing tricks. It was entertainment.

Why aren't more miracles recorded in the Bible? Because the Bible isn't meant to be entertainment. Sure, you can read it and learn from it and enjoy it; you'll even find some funny moments. But the writers wanted to show that Jesus didn't come to do tricks, and he didn't come to do miracles; he came to save us. The ultimate miracle—the only one that really matters—is salvation. Jesus died and came back from the dead for us.

If you are praying to God to see a miracle, then make sure you are looking for a miracle. Maybe the miracle will be that your dog begins to float in midair and bark "Amazing Grace," but more than likely the miracle will be spiritual. It will be the presence of God in your life.

The problem with seeking miracles is that we seek them all wrong. We seek miracles to answer our physical, earthly problems: "God, if you're there, if you are real, then find me a job . . . heal my medical condition . . . give me money."

If you want a miracle, then recognize that the miracle is not an object or a thing or even a healing. A miracle is the presence of God in your life. Seek his presence, thank him for his presence, worship him—and watch the miracles pour forth. Watch what God does in your life. Be thankful for the bad and the good. Be thankful because there is no moment, even bad, when God is not present.

There's nothing wrong with asking for a miracle—never stop asking for it. If you are sick and want to be healed, then ask to be healed. Have your friends ask. Have your pastor ask. Have the random stranger ask for it! And never stop asking for it until the miracle is given. But don't look for the physical healing—look for the spiritual healing. Look for God's presence, and see what he is doing not to physically heal you but to spiritually heal you. Maybe your spiritual healing will also be a physical one. Or maybe it won't—but God is still with you, and he is revealing things to you. Trust and follow him.

Getting Social

Twitter: Tweet about something random and miraculous that happened recently in your life: #spiritualmiracle.

Pinterest: Create a board called "Miracle" full of clippings of various books and websites about miracles.

Instagram: Take a picture of something that makes you aware of God's presence: #MiraclesHappen.

LinkedIn: Add "Miracle Worker" as a job skill. If anyone asks, tell them you are the go-to guy for helping people find God's presence.

Facebook: Post on your wall about something small that could only be one thing: the presence of God.

WhichBibleHero AreYou?

Which movie would you most likely watch?

A. *Il Postino* (+1)

B. *Clueless* (+3)

C. *Old Yeller* (+5)

D. *American President* (+7)

E. *UHF* (+9)

F. *Pretty Woman* (+11)

Commercial Break

Interview with an Atheist

I t's not uncommon for books to have two parts. The problem is, the parts are usually only divided by page breaks. There's nothing jarring to indicate that both the tone and themes have changed.

In this self-titled commercial, we will read an AMA[1] between Roland, who is an atheist, and me. There are no rebuttals here—just answers.

I hope you don't fast-forward through the interview, but if you do, that's fine.

SCOTT: In another book-based interview, you talked about wearing shoes that you "believed" were from the brand Alfani. What are you wearing these days?

---

1. Ask Me Anything

ROLAND: Converse low-tops and black Nike sneakers, depending on how fancy I want to feel.

SCOTT: What caused you to switch shoes?

ROLAND: Nothing. I just put them on my feet and get on with life.

SCOTT: When we first met, you were known to carry around a notebook full of notes on procedure. Have you ever referred back to them?

ROLAND: Maybe a couple of times during the first month I worked there [at the library]. I quickly learned that aside from a couple of passwords, I could forget everything I wrote down and still do fine.

SCOTT: What is your favorite theology-driven episode of the Simpsons?

ROLAND: Probably "Homer the Heretic."

SCOTT: What do you think of biblical epics?

ROLAND: I love them. They're almost like superhero films, but with God.

SCOTT: What do you think about the new pope?

ROLAND: Love him. He's not as liberal as people are claiming, but he's definitely a step in the right direction.

SCOTT: Have you ever paused and said, "Maybe this religion is true?"

ROLAND: Maybe years ago, but definitely not recently.

SCOTT: What's the weirdest thing a Christian has ever done
            to convert you?

ROLAND: Some wordplay years ago when I said I was agnostic.
            They basically took the word apart and said, "Oh,
            so you mean you know nothing?" Not sure why this
            was supposed to convert me. If anything, it made me
            dig in my heels further.

SCOTT: Who was the most spiritual person you have ever
            known (Christian or non-Christian)? What made
            them spiritual?

ROLAND: No one really stands out. I've known some great
            people who are religious, but there's not one shining
            example that I can hold up or anything.

SCOTT: What was faith like as a child?

ROLAND: Nonexistent for the most part. I was baptized and we
            celebrated the holidays, but we never went to church
            or anything. The only specific thing I remember
            about my faith from when I was younger was curling
            up on the couch and crying because I couldn't stop
            thinking about hell. That feeling probably influenced
            my later views on religion in general.

SCOTT: When was the last time you went into a church for
            a service—excluding things like weddings, commu-
            nion, etcetera?

ROLAND: When I was in high school and some friends con-
            vinced me to go. I saw a friend go up and start

speaking in tongues. That was when I realized this wasn't for me.

SCOTT: What was your process of unbelief—from agnostic to atheism, that is? Did any writer or person influence it, or was it more of a personal thought process?

ROLAND: Richard Dawkins's book *The God Delusion* answered some nagging questions that I had about faith, but studying the history of the Latter-day Saints pushed me over the edge into full-on atheism. Here is a major world religion with newspaper accounts and a mountain of primary sources detailing its founding, and there's no possible way that it could be true. Over 15 million people put their faith in a religion where the facts surrounding the writing of the holy text and the historical information detailed therein can easily be proven false. Why should I believe older stories just because the sources are no longer available?

SCOTT: If there is no God, who defines moral code?

ROLAND: We do.

SCOTT: While not believing in it, you used to have a lot of love for the Mormon church. Is that still the case?

ROLAND: I'm not as fanatical in my excitement, but I still love it.

SCOTT: What drew you to it?

ROLAND: It was the first time I'd heard of a major religion with a complete written record of its founding, right from the beginning. And not just from believers, but from newspapers and journals at the time. It's remarkable to see how a religion is formed. It was also probably the one thing that completely moved me over into atheism more than anything else.

SCOTT: Do you think any Mormon leaders saw visions? Or do you think they made the visions up?

ROLAND: I think some may have seen visions, but since Mormons are told to listen for that small, still voice, this is just part of their faith. If you really believe something hard enough, you can force it into being.

SCOTT: Why do you think the Mormon church spread so rapidly?

ROLAND: It put Jesus in the United States. That's an incredibly appealing idea for an American.

SCOTT: Why do you think people join cults?

ROLAND: For the same reason people convert to religion. Everyone wants an answer or to belong to a group.

SCOTT: Your answers to some of these questions might seem a little self-explanatory, but just so everyone understands what an atheist is (and isn't)—at least where the term applies to you—I'm going to ask them anyway.

ROLAND: Okay.

SCOTT: Do you believe in demons?

ROLAND: Just the personal ones, like drinking and other
           addictions.

SCOTT: If there is a God, do you think there is also a hell
           where people are eternally damned?

ROLAND: No. If a God exists, I would like to think that an
           ugly human trait like revenge doesn't factor into his
           decisions.

SCOTT: Do you believe in miracles?

ROLAND: No.

SCOTT: Do you believe in divine intervention?

ROLAND: No.

SCOTT: Has anything ever happened to you that you cannot
           explain—to the point where you questioned if it was
           divine intervention?

ROLAND: Anything that might have that kind of appearance
           I've chalked up to luck.

SCOTT: If you were dying of some affliction and a person
           prayed over you and you were no longer sick—luck
           still?

ROLAND: Prayer works all the time, just like sugar pills.
           People can make themselves sick just by believing it
           hard enough. If I were egotistical enough to think
           that God would swoop down to save me while he
           saw fit to chill out on his cloud while things like

the Holocaust and the Black Plague happened, that would probably say more about me than it would God.

SCOTT: Have you ever read the Bible in its entirety?

ROLAND: Just Genesis. I've been meaning to read the rest. I have, however, read the Book of Mormon, and man, was that a slog to get through.

SCOTT: Is there anything in the Bible that would make you not believe in it simply because it's dumb?

ROLAND: Perhaps the book of Job, but really, these are stories, and I think most of it is to be taken as metaphor.

SCOTT: Do you think Leviticus-type laws helped or hurt Jews?

ROLAND: They might have helped at the time. They probably don't do a whole lot of good now.

SCOTT: Non-holy text included, what do you think is the greatest "religious" book?

ROLAND: Can't think of one, but that's probably because I need to read more books. Most of my favorites don't seem to operate from a religious angle aside from bucking against it, like *Portrait of the Artist as a Young Man*.

SCOTT: Is heaven real?

ROLAND: No.

SCOTT: What do you think Christians need to believe to go
            to heaven?

ROLAND: I don't think Christians need to believe anything;
            they just need to treat people right and live good
            lives. There are too many things in the Bible that
            contradict each other that I don't think God would
            pick and choose and then deny someone entry
            because they missed one.

SCOTT: If you are wrong, and there is a heaven, what do you
            think it looks like?

ROLAND: If there's a heaven, it probably looks like nothing
            I've ever seen before or can imagine. Our minds are
            limited, and I don't think heaven would look like
            something as boring as a bunch of clouds.

SCOTT: What happens when we die?

ROLAND: The same thing that happened before we were con-
            ceived, I'd imagine.

SCOTT: Does death scare you?

ROLAND: Sometimes, but that's mainly because I don't know
            what happens next.

SCOTT: Do you believe there has to be something, some-
            where that is eternal—with no beginning and no
            end, that created all?

ROLAND: No. That seems too much like projecting human
            traits onto something random in the universe. I do

think that our minds are limited and can only conceive a finite set of ideas, so who knows?

SCOTT: If scientists developed a way to keep the organs alive forever, would you want to live forever?

ROLAND: No. At some point I'm going to get old and set in my ways, and I won't view things the way I do now. If I lived forever I'd probably spend the rest of my life complaining about how things aren't like they used to be.

SCOTT: Do you think science will ever evolve to the point where it can say how the universe began?

ROLAND: I think we can only have theories. We'll never really know for sure.

SCOTT: What do you think the point of life is?

ROLAND: I think, at a basic level, the only point of all life is to continue life—so reproduction. But people who either can't or won't reproduce aren't failing at life. I don't understand the meaning of life, I just try to make sense of it based on what I know. Reproduction makes the most sense to me.

SCOTT: Atheists will admit that they don't believe in God because you can't prove God, but many will also admit there is life on other planets. Do you think much of modern atheism comes from a grudge for how religion has treated science?

ROLAND: First, I think that atheists grant that there may be life on other planets, not that there definitely is. The loud, vocal atheists definitely operate from a grudge, but honestly, they have every reason to. For example, there is absolutely no reason why evolution should be banned from schools or why creationism should be taught alongside it. You would never hear an atheist say that our point of view should be taught in church.

SCOTT: If life was discovered on another planet, do you think there would be the existence of some form of religion? Like, is it in the foundations of man to believe in something beyond their own understanding?

ROLAND: Religion seems uniquely human. Plus if life exists elsewhere, we have no clue what kind of life it is.

SCOTT: Do you think a scientist who is Christian would receive some amount of bias for his or her belief before their theory is even heard?

ROLAND: No.

SCOTT: In your opinion, who is the most absurd Christian?

ROLAND: Kirk Cameron. Which reminds me, I heard that his [last] *Left Behind* film was more entertaining than the new one. I haven't seen the new one, so I can't verify this claim.

SCOTT: Do you believe he believes in Christ, or do you believe it is all a show?

ROLAND: I have no doubt that he's sincere.

SCOTT: Did you ever play the *Left Behind* video game?

ROLAND: I didn't even know this existed, but now I want to
                play it.

SCOTT: Do you think Christianity has a higher ratio of crazy
                people than other religions? Why do you think that
                is or isn't?

ROLAND: No. Every religion has their extremists. Christians
                are more media-savvy, though, so your Kirk
                Camerons really stand out.

SCOTT: A lot of Christians whine about becoming the
                minority voice. Do you believe there's any truth to
                this?

ROLAND: I believe that they believe it, in the same way that the
                US still views itself as the "underdog." They think
                there's this huge atheist conspiracy, but there are so
                few of us here that it's ridiculous to assume that we
                have enough clout to destroy Christmas or whatever
                they think we're plotting.

SCOTT: What do you think would happen if more Christians
                converted to Christianity and became more Christian?
                Would it affect your own faith at all?

ROLAND: It wouldn't affect my faith because it's not a choice
                for me. With how I view the world, religion doesn't
                figure into it.

SCOTT: Do you think Christianity will only decrease in
                numbers?

ROLAND: It's possible. No religion stays on top forever.

SCOTT: Do any religions outright scare you? And why?

ROLAND: Not one in particular, but fundamentalism is
           terrifying.

SCOTT: Do you think there's too much hypersensitiv-
           ity regarding religion and school on both sides of
           spectrum?

ROLAND: No. Too many religious folks with agendas are
           trying to force their beliefs into textbooks that are
           taught to students as fact. This is a serious issue and
           I don't think people are overreacting at all to it. This
           is a big thing that atheists have every right to be
           angry about.

SCOTT: Why does the very idea of religion make so many
           people emotional and even angry?

ROLAND: Nobody likes being told they're wrong.

SCOTT: Do you feel threatened by Christians at times?

ROLAND: Not yet, but wait until I have kids and have to put
           them in school.

SCOTT: Do you ever feel threatened by atheists?

ROLAND: No. We're not nearly as militant as people assume.

SCOTT: How would you define religion?

ROLAND: The belief in a divine force that governs life accord-
            ing to certain rules.

SCOTT: Do you think atheism is becoming a religion of
            sorts?

ROLAND: No. All religions, every single one of them, operate
            on faith. Atheism doesn't work that way. The closest
            thing to an atheist religion that you can find are cults
            and people like Ayn Rand fans, who think there is
            one single divine truth and view the world through
            that only.

SCOTT: What separates you from a Christian? Are we
            essentially the same person—despite the fact that a
            Christian believes in Christ? Or do you see anything
            else that differentiates between the two?

ROLAND: I think that we both try to do what's right and treat
            others fairly. The big differences come in how we
            deal with loss and grieving, I suppose.

SCOTT: If God is real, why do you think there is pain and
            suffering?

ROLAND: I guess you can't appreciate joy unless you feel pain.
            Other than that, I don't know.

SCOTT: Do you believe Christ existed?

ROLAND: Yes.

SCOTT: Do you believe he did miracles?

ROLAND: No.

SCOTT: What happened to his body?

ROLAND: If he was a revolutionary at the time, he was proba-
             bly buried with other criminals and undesirables. He
             was crucified alongside a couple of thieves, right?

SCOTT: What would it take for you to believe in God?

ROLAND: Probably something bombastic, like a gigantic hand
             coming out of the sky. I've seen things that a lot of
             people probably imagine are ghosts, but it's usually
             just a brief trick of light. There's this view of atheists
             that we're just stubborn and don't want to just let
             go and believe. The truth is, again, I can't believe it.
             I would have to ignore too much of what I already
             know, disregard too many things. It would be harder
             for me to convert to a religion than probably any-
             thing else because I just can't do it. It's a "one plus
             one equals three" type of deal for me.

And now, back to your normal book viewing.

Part Two

Not Yo Mama's Faith

Chapter Eight

Natura-Diddily

#SorrowIsLonely

Bad things happen.

We know this because we have Facebook.[1] We see stories all the time: Heartwarming posts. Tragic posts. Sad little posts that somehow put a smile on your face. I guarantee you that nobody who hurts has ever felt better because someone liked his or her post about hardship. A billion likes will not take pain away.

It's fair to say that everyone has seen some form of the "Footprints in the Sand" allegory, which is basically about God carrying a person during the hardships. It's an allegory worthy of a Facebook post and a million likes. It's so warm and fuzzy. But it says absolutely

---

1. Can someone please get little Timmy a million "likes" so he can die peacefully?

nothing to a person who is suffering. Bad things happen, and when they do, nothing is warm, fuzzy, or cute about it. It hurts.

Some people live their whole life quite uneventfully—a death here and there, and maybe a bad bruise. Other people live a little too eventfully—years of suffering, trials, and hardships.

For the better part of my preteen and teenage years, I wore a back brace. I was one of the lucky few males who had severe scoliosis. The brace was supposed to help keep my back from curving, but after years of growth, I was told at the age of fifteen that if I didn't have surgery, my outlook would be less than ideal. A growth spurt had caused my spine to curve more than anticipated, and it had begun to curve into my lungs. I was already experiencing the effects; my lung capacity was on par with someone who had been smoking two packs a day for most of their life.

It wasn't supposed to be like this. Teens were supposed to play sports, go on dates, and learn to drive, not have spinal surgery. Not have to take deeper breaths because their lungs were working in overdrive. But I didn't question God. I didn't know that was an option.

The summer prior to my junior year of high school, I had the surgery. Over the course of about ten hours, two rods were inserted into my back, and bone marrow taken from my hip fused the rods into my spine. The surgery went without a hitch, but a few days later, my lungs collapsed and I was put on a ventilator.

When I finally left the hospital, there was a long road still ahead of me. Walking even to the bathroom was a chore; it took months before I started feeling somewhat normal and over a year before I was fully recovered.

But I didn't question God's authority.

For years, I would look back and feel like this was my great trial—the tragic event that most of us are bound to experience in some form.[2]

Throughout the entire ordeal, only one person my age visited me. The youth minister had forgotten I was in the hospital, but he had

---

2. Spoiler Alert: It was not.

the youth group sign a card a few weeks later. A few of them even got my name right.

I didn't mind. Even in my youth, I knew I was different. I believed in a different kind of Jesus than other teens. They believed in a cool Jesus; I believed in the Jesus of rejects. It was fitting that the only person who visited me was a reject just like me.

When I left this ordeal, I felt like I'd had my trial and had overcome. Life could now resume and be happily ever after. But this trial was more like crumbs off the table next to the trial that was yet to come.

WikiBreak

"Footprints in the Sand" has many variants, but all are essentially the same. They tell of a time where a person is walking on the beach with God, leaving two sets of footprints. But as time goes on, the man (or woman) goes through trials. Looking back, he sees only one set of footprints and questions why God abandoned him. That's when the story turns weepy. God tells the man that during the hard times, those were the times when God carried him.

So where did the poem come from? It's tricky to say.

The phenomenon the poem describes is something quite old called the Third Man Factor.

The late great preacher Charles Spurgeon delivered a sermon in 1901 titled "The Education of Sons of God" in which he talked about footprints in the sand that clearly belonged to Jesus (because they had nail prints in them). Many point to this as the earliest version of the story. That's doubtful, however.

The idea of the footprints, while cute, is also a little generic. During the last fifty years, over a dozen people have claimed authorship—and why not? There's literally millions of dollars in licensing to collect if a copyright can be proven. The trouble is, copyright can't be proven. Anyone can write their own version of the poem and copyright it, but nobody can copyright the actual idea of footprints in the sand.

Sometimes pain happens as a result of our personal sin. Other times it is due to someone else's actions. And still other times, pain is God's means of teaching us a lesson. All three categories of pain hurt, but it helps to know there's a reason behind them.

That's all neat and tidy, but there's a fourth kind of pain that's harder to handle because it can't be pinned down. There's no reason for it, no satisfactory answers for why it happens. It just happens—and it hurts.

Disclaimer: The next scene is a little messy. If you need to believe that bad things don't happen to good people, or that bad things happen to good people for a divine reason, then this is where you stop reading and jump to the next chapter.

For forty weeks, I watched the miracle of pregnancy. I watched my wife's body do things that made no sense. One of the best evidences of God is pregnancy; it's as if a woman's body defies all logic to deliver what should otherwise be impossible. It's called the "miracle of life" for a reason: science cannot completely explain all the things that happen to a woman's body to make it occur.

But then everything changed. Life stopped.

We went for a routine stress test because Diana was just a few days past her delivery date. The test told us quite bluntly that all was not well. The heartbeat that had been so strong a mere three days before was no longer there.

Denial hit first. I did not believe our baby could be gone. He was just hiding. But more testing confirmed it. Our baby boy was dead.

When the first of many waves of tears had passed, I thought of Jesus's promise that if we have faith in God, we can tell a mountain to move to the sea, and the request will be granted.[3] As labor was induced and we waited over a day for the baby to come out, that was all I could think of. The child would be our miracle baby. I

---

3. Matthew 21:21.

believed. I believed that God could give him life again, that his heart would beat again, that it was all a mistake. But it didn't happen.

When babies are born, it's a natural process. The mom and the child work together. The birth of a stillborn is a bit trickier. In the end, our son was nearly pulled out of my wife. I was not angry with God, but it was unbearable to look at what should have been living, crying, and not question why. As we said our last good-bye to him and his earthly body was removed from the room, a new life had begun for us—not the joyous adventure of parenthood, but a journey of mourning.

A few weeks later, someone, thinking it might make us feel better, sent a story to us about a dead baby who came back to life when it was held to its mother's chest. Not surprisingly, the story did not make either of us feel better; all we could think was, why did this not happen for us?

We were now the unfortunate new members of a club of people who understand firsthand that warm, fuzzy stories and trite mottos just don't make grieving people feel good. The Bible doesn't say that bad things happen for a reason. The Bible doesn't say things will get better. It doesn't say a lot of things. It didn't promise us a new baby.

When something like that happens, you don't just experience grief—you experience despair. Grief occurs when your grandparents or parents die at a respectable age; it occurs when sad things that are supposed to happen, happen. It's hard. You are sad. But you get through it.

But when you experience despair, a part of your soul leaves you and you don't get it back. You get through it; you move on the best you can. But for the rest of your life, you're aware of something that should be there but is not.

And nothing can comfort you in that.

The only true comfort is knowing why it happened, but that is something you can never know on earth. One day, you will sit with God in heaven and understand. But on earth, all you can do is get to the point where you accept that you will never know the answer.

There is a point where you can see the good in the bad, a time when you can look at what you went through and see there were positive things. But none of them will ever justify the loss you have experienced.

When you finally get past "Why?" to the acceptance stage, you have to face another question that is equally hard: What now? How do you move on from tragedy? It's easy to experience the presence of God when times are good, but if you really want to experience the presence of God, then wait for it all to come crashing down.

Just like before, I felt God's presence with me, but I did not feel the church's presence. Once again, the church had let me down. But that was okay, because my wife and I had accepted long ago that this is a fact of life: the church will let you down. We were fortunate to be strong enough in our faith not to believe in the church, but to believe beyond the church in Jesus Christ.

Fearful of saying the wrong things, people often choose to say nothing. But the worst thing to say to someone grieving is nothing at all. Even when you say the wrong thing, that person will find comfort knowing that when others were quiet, you were strong enough to care.

In our own experience, the people my wife and I expected to be there were gone, but people we never imagined would be there for us showered us with love. It's said that proof of God is often found in the grace of the believers. This is true, but grace can be found in unbelievers too. This was certainly the case with us.

The presence of suffering doesn't mean the absence of God. Jesus never says belief in God will be the road to a happy life. Happiness was not Jesus's ministry—salvation was. His promise is the presence of God during trials.

A lot of televangelists—a lot of ministers in general—preach that if you pray hard enough or give enough money, you will be rich, ill-free, and happy. These preachers are often wildly successful, because people want to believe in good things. We know that bad things happen, but we are also in denial of it; it's much easier to live tuning that stuff out.

Our minds have been fed this gospel of prosperity so often that we aren't always equipped to handle bad things when they come our way. If we follow God, we are not promised wealth; we are not promised health; we are not promised material happiness at all.

On the contrary, the Bible promises one thing: hardship. And Hebrews 12:7 tells us we should endure that hardship as discipline. That's not exactly the rags-to-riches verse a lot of us hope for.

In 2 Corinthians 12, Paul writes about his own hardship, which he described as a thorn placed in his flesh. Scholars have debated what this thorn was for hundreds of years, but it really doesn't matter; what matters is what God tells Paul about the thorn. In verse 9, he says, "My grace is sufficient for you, for my power is made perfect in weakness."

USELESS POLL

When bad things happen, I . . .
- A. pray and become closer to God.
- B. become angry.
- C. reject God's love.
- D. demand answers.

To be part of this poll, visit:
www.OrganicJesus.com/useless-polls

In hard times, I frequently turn to this verse. I don't know why things happen the way they happen, but a part of me rejoices when they happen, for they bring me closer to God. The times when I have felt closest to God were the times when I felt like I was at rock bottom. Neither my wife nor I rejoiced at the death of our son, but it did not take us long to be able to have joy in the closeness to God that we felt.

With enough work, you can achieve wealth. With the right diet and exercise, you can have health. With the right mind-set, you can have earthly happiness. But only in Christ can you have salvation.

Most people get uncomfortable when bad things happen to others. They sympathize, but they would prefer to simply send a card and be on their merry way.

On the other extreme, there's a group that clings to tragedy, people who morbidly want to hear about it just so they can gossip about their friend who experienced something horrible. They're easy to spot. They're the person who has a tragic story to share in every situation. You say, "I had the best breakfast burrito," and the person tells you about a friend who choked on the sausage in her breakfast burrito and wound up in the emergency room, where she learned by chance that she had a rare brain disease and would be dead in a week.

I don't believe these people enjoy the suffering of others, but knowing that people suffer makes them appreciate their own lives more.

One thing can help the brokenhearted, and that's compassion. Not listening to their story so you can share it with someone else. Not ignoring their story because it reminds you of death. Simply showing compassion.

Just as people asked my wife and me what the worst thing was to say to someone grieving, people also asked what the best thing was. That, too, was an easy answer: I'm sorry.

Grieving people don't need empathy; they need sympathy. They need the presence of love. They need people who will take the time to listen and to shed a few tears themselves.

Actions speak louder than cards. So don't be afraid to show your presence.

A lot of people told me, "If you need anything at all, just ask." We're programmed to say it. But if a person is going through something bad enough to warrant the standard "If you need anything" phrase, then they are probably not going to ask. They need people to just act. Helpless people don't ask for help. When you are in a state of helplessness, you are numb to your own needs. You are doing the bare minimum to survive.

Let's do a little exercise for a moment. Open your Bible to the Gospels[4] and count all the passages where Jesus is seen asking people, "What can I do to help you?"

---

4. Hint: They're a little more than halfway through your Bible.

Finished? Not a lot, right?

Christ saw a need and acted on it. It wasn't because he was God—because he had superpowers to read inside the minds of the hurting, and give them what they needed. Christ *was* (and is) God; he *did* (and does) have superpowers. But it doesn't take superpowers to see a person hurting and know they need love.

We say we are called to follow Christ, but we have trouble following him in this matter of simply acting on the needs of others. We want the person to give us permission to love them. For some reason, we feel like grief is a sensitive topic. It's not! Grief is the one topic we should be loud about. We should hear stories about people becoming Christians because they saw the sheer love poured out on grieving people.

As much as I would love to know why bad things happen, I simply can't. If God is trying to teach me something from the death of my son, I don't know what it is, and believe me I've listened. All I hear is silence.

While love helps the brokenhearted, grief nevertheless hurts. It changes you. There's a darkness that seems to loom forever. How can God create something as extreme as grief? Why give us something that makes us feel lonely, lost, terrified, and downright sad? I used to believe that tragedies happened for a reason, but I can't believe that anymore. Only God can know.

"If there is a God, then why do bad things happen?" I think that's really not the question for Christians to ask. We should ask, "If God lives through me, then how can I help the person who has had something bad happen?"

It doesn't take the presence of grief to experience the presence of God. It only takes love. Love the hurting and the Spirit will surely move through you.

Getting Social

Twitter: Tweet about a time when you felt the presence of God in hardship: #JoyfulPain.

Pinterest: Create a board called "Hardship," full of articles and pictures of Christians getting through tragedy by the grace of God.

Instagram: Find a person who is in need. Don't ask what they need—act. Put your phone away; don't capture the moment. Some moments are best remembered with your heart.

LinkedIn: Reach out to a friend who has lost his job and do something to help. You don't have to find him a job—help comes in many forms.

Facebook: Find a friend who has posted something about a hardship. Now put away your computer and call or visit that person. Bonus points: Do something that shows unexpected love.

Which Bible Hero Are You?

Which is your ideal cell phone?

A. An Apple iPhone (+1)

B. A flip phone (+3)

C. The brand I've had all my life (+5)

D. A Blackberry (+7)

E. A banana (+9)

F. An Android (+11)

Chapter Nine

Would Jesus Take a Selfie?

#HeavenlySelfie

I was raised in a Methodist church in Orange County, California. Orange County is everything you'd imagine in a setting with perfect weather and a beach as one of its borders. It's casual—flip-flops and shorts were common even at expensive restaurants. Everyone tries either surfing or skateboarding at some point. And if you stay there long enough, you are bound to come face-to-face with a celebrity or two[2] and have a skin cancer scare or two.[3]

Despite the casualness of the county, it always stopped at church.

---

1. Jesus using an old-school digital camera to get his selfie on.
2. My most memorable encounter was with Screech from *Saved by the Bell.*
3. I'm going on about a dozen of those.

Church was something you dressed up for; when you walked into a church, there was always a feeling of sacredness. At least in my youth.

A milestone for all youths in the church was when they reached the age when they could become acolytes.[4] When I was in fifth grade, my time came. My training began with a dinner with other would-be acolytes at the home of Mrs. Smith, a widowed woman who exemplified the sacred and profane.

She was a woman I had known of for most of my childhood—a prominent figure in the church. It wasn't until I was in her home, though, that I got to know her thirsty secret. More than a strong hint of liquor could be smelled on the breath of Mrs. Smith as she explained the expectations of an acolyte to the group of new recruits that sat on her living room sofa.

Had I been older, I would have observed to myself the irony of the whiskey-drinking woman explaining how the fire we brought into the church to light the candle represented the light of Christ. But I was not older. I was not even a teen, and while I grasped the holiness of the ritual, mostly I understood that there would be cake after the explanation.

There were lots of unmentionables with the woman's family, none of which could be openly addressed, only whispered about. She was a respectable church figure and had to look saintly. Perhaps she turned to the bottle because it was the only thing in her life that gave her comfort.

WikiBreak

Millions of Christians have fallen, some harder than others. Below is a list of some that you may have never heard of who gave Christianity a bad name in the process.

---

4. The person who performed the ceremonial duty of lighting the altar candles at our Methodist church. Once the candles were lit, the acolyte essentially became the minister's assistant during the duration of the service. He sat next to the minister, and if the minister needed water or anything else, he'd call on the acolyte to fetch it.

AD 50-ish

Ananias and Sapphira were two very early members of the Christian church. They are remembered more for what they did than who they were. In Acts 5, an account is given of each of them instantly dying after lying to the apostles about money. It was probably the first real scandal of the church following Christ's resurrection. People to this day continue to argue about why they had to die.

1609-ish

The Baptist church we know today started in a place not often thought of when we think of Baptist: Amsterdam. While it has no single creator, many cite John Smyth as its most prominent figure. Smyth rejected baptism of infants, and a movement was born that quickly began to spread. Smyth first baptized himself and then began baptizing other adults. But not long after the movement began taking off, Smyth had a change of heart. He decided that baptizing did not count, and he left the movement he was largely responsible for starting. He began the process of becoming a member of the Mennonite church, but died before his membership went through. Many of his followers became Mennonites as well.

1926

In the 1920s and 30s, Aimee Semple McPherson, also known as Sister Aimee, was a rock star in the Christian community. For a time, she was one of the most known figures in the country. Married three times, Sister Aimee could never be considered a saint in the love territory, but it was another story that rocked her legacy. In 1926, Sister Aimee went out for a swim at the beach—and disappeared. She was almost immediately presumed dead by drowning.

Soon ransom notes began showing up at Sister Aimee's church. They were, for the most part, just considered hoaxes. Then over a month after her alleged death, she stumbled out of the Arizona desert and claimed she had been drugged and kidnapped, but had managed to escape and make a thirteen-hour trek through the desert. The trouble was, some considered the condition of her health and her clothing to be too good to fit her ordeal. Witnesses soon began popping up claiming they had seen her in various places. Reasons for her disappearance varied widely; abortion, publicity, and plastic surgery were all popular rumors. In the end, whether she had told the truth or a lie remained unknown.

1940s

Few Christians would argue that the Nazis were right; unfortunately, "few" means that some in fact believed they were. While there are stories of Christians helping Jewish people hide, others tell of Christians who assisted the Nazi party. Two notable examples:

Robert Alesch: A French priest who worked as an intelligence agent for the Nazi party. Under his actions, dozens of people, if not hundreds, were tortured by the Germans. He was executed by firing squad in 1949.

Jozef Tiso: While anti-Semitism in the Nazi Party is typically linked to Hitler, many in the party helped make it happen. One of the biggest leaders was Jozef Tiso, a Roman Catholic priest who helped with the deportation of thousands of Jews. For his role, he was hanged in 1947.

It's unfortunate, but as you mature in faith you will most likely experience one (or more likely several) Christians who truly disappoint you. I'm not talking about a televangelist who is caught up in a scandal—those guys are a dime a dozen. I'm talking about a person who meant something to you—a person you even looked up to. But then they did something that was not only un-Christian but also not very human.

The thing that has always drawn me to Christianity is not the religion that has shaped it, but the theology that created it. The fact is, flawed figures are not uniquely Christian; sex scandals—money scandals—murder scandals—they are found in all faiths. Humans are flawed and it should shock no one when someone screws up. Christianity is about the forgiveness of man's inability to be perfect, not the quest to do nothing wrong.

Christianity isn't a religion about you. It's a religion about them. It's a religion that says, Look beyond yourself. Look beyond what you feel. Look beyond those who have hurt you. Look beyond all of that to others who are hurting. You are already saved, but those hurting people—they mean so much to God. And he wants to use you as a vessel to heal them.

We are a culture of selfies. All of us have Googled ourselves more than we'd care to admit, because we want to know what people think of us. One of the world's biggest websites—Facebook, the one many of us use for communication more than even email—revolves around one phrase: "What's on *your* mind?" It's a place for us to share our feelings, frustrations, news, anger, etc.

There's nothing wrong with any of these things—until we let something be wrong with them. Until we let ourselves take the place of God. Until we become a culture so involved with our own lives that we don't see the lives around us. Until we think the only way to help a person is by posting encouragement through a text message instead of giving a hug.

If Jesus had walked the earth today rather than two thousand years ago, I highly doubt he'd be on Facebook; I doubt he'd have a cell phone; and I seriously doubt he'd Google himself. Because Jesus Christ isn't Internet friendly. The entire ministry of Christ was based on actions that couldn't be captured on YouTube; it had to be seen firsthand, so you'd be motivated to tell others.

If Jesus's ministry was so large, then how come more people didn't talk about it? Because it actually wasn't that big. There were a few thousand followers, but that's nothing compared to today. The reason Christianity spread was not by the miracles; it was by the believers. It was because Christ ministered in a way that made his followers follow suit.

So when I hear about people who are hurt for being wronged by a believer, I can't help but wonder if their perspective is all wrong. They should be more concerned with helping people than being hurt by them.

People love to take religion buffet style, a little here and a little there. If a person doesn't like something, then they can just ignore it and even find a Bible verse or two to support why they've done so. But when we start picking and choosing what we like and don't like, something happens: things fall apart. You can't say, "I love this house, but I hate the wall. Let's just take it out." When you remove a wall, the roof comes down. You can't live in a house like that.

Christianity is a mess. Christians are messy. And that's okay. God doesn't call us to believe in the religion. He calls us to believe in Jesus.

Throughout the New Testament, you can tell there's a debate going on: there are Christians who believe we must do good works to be saved. That's one hundred percent false. Through Christ, we do good works, but those works aren't what save us. Yet even today people argue the point. The idea that believing in Christ is all it takes to be saved completely baffles some. That's how cults get started. People want rules, and they follow sects that say, "If you do this, this, and this, then you are saved."

But there's only one way, one path to salvation, and it has absolutely nothing to do with who you are, what you've done, or what you do. It has nothing to do with your sins, and it has nothing to do with your lifestyle. It has nothing to do with any of that. It has everything to do with your heart and who it believes is Lord.

It's odd that we're the only mammals who still drink milk after we're infants. Maybe this is a statement on mankind, how we are never really off the bottle. Humans are a strange beast that never quite grows up and stops being a kid. We are a creature that prowls in cycles of maturity and immaturity.

There was a time when I was mature. Then I slipped. Now I feel, finally, that I'm becoming the person I once was. But soon there will come a new cycle when I must learn a new maturity. The point is, we never do grow up; we're always learning how to cure ourselves of this constant cycle of immaturity.

In Hebrews 5:13, the author writes of this idea of milk when he says, "Anyone who lives on milk, being still an infant, is not acquainted with the teaching about righteousness." What the author is referring to are people who haven't ever been through the cycle of maturity and immaturity, people who are stuck in a constant state of infancy. They have never gotten to a stage in their lives where they feel they have grown and are a changed person. There are many people like this—many. People who accept Christ but are just never quite able to progress from there.

At what point do we grow? We grow at the point where the Spirit has not just entered our body but has taken control of our body—when we surrender ourselves, and admit that peace only can come when we trust that he is in control of our life. Many Christians are stuck. They accepted God, and the Spirit now lives within them, but he is constrained. Life goes on as normal; the only difference is, now those persons say they are Christians.

A lot of churches talk about people's need to "get fed." The fact is, there are a lot of overweight Christians. They don't need to get fed—they need to teach. Church should be focused on getting believers to a point of maturity where they are teachers, passing down the sacred rites of the church.

Christianity is a religion of mentorship, but this age is one that lacks mentors. We're so stuck on making ourselves better that we forget that it's not about us.

To many people, mentorship is about creating a person in our own image, teaching them how we have become who we are. That strategy of mentorship may work great in business, but in Christianity, mentorship needs to be about helping people connect with God.

Mentorship doesn't begin with us. It doesn't begin with another person. It begins with God.

Getting Social

Twitter: Tweet about an unlikely person of influence in your life: #HeavenlySelfie.

Pinterest: Create a board called "Mentors" full of people around the world who can teach us a thing or two.

Instagram: Take a picture of someone you admire or look up to: #HeavenlySelfie.

LinkedIn: Add "mentor" as a job skill. Count how many people endorse the skill.

Facebook: Post about someone who helped you mature in faith. Bonus points if you tag them in a picture. Encourage people to comment on whom they look up to and who has helped them grow.

Which Bible Hero Are You?

What kind of shoes do you wear?

A. Tap dancing or ballet shoes (+1)

B. Sneakers (+3)

C. The brand I've worn all my life (+5)

D. Something that can be polished (+7)

E. Shoes? I don't need shoes. (+9)

F. Stilettos or army boots (+11)

ChapterTen

Love in a Time of Cholera

#IsChristianityBroken

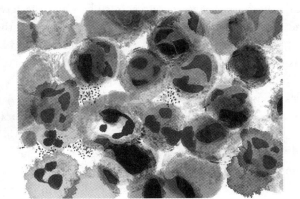

The Jews killed Jesus. Muslims killed everyone else, and we have an entire crusade to prove it.

That statement is, of course, not true, but that doesn't stop people from hating. For such a loving religion, Christianity has harbored an awful lot of hate. In theory, the kind of hate seen across the world today goes against every principle in the New Testament. But revenge is in our DNA. When someone wrongs us, it's an eye for an eye. Never mind the Bible. Or mind the Bible only when it's practical, as some Christians would have us believe.

People have said the Bible is full of contradictions. That's not true: people are full of contradictions. They speak one thing with their lips but believe something entirely different with their hearts. In the end, actions speak louder than words, and in the case of Christians, their actions are unfortunately not always very Christian.

Why the hate? You can play the "Christians are flawed" card for only so long. At some point you have to pause and say, "Really, people, you just need to stop it! If you are really a Christian, then no more hate."

Jews may have been present at the persecution of Jesus, but you can hardly say that all Jews were responsible. Only the Jewish religious and political leaders were guilty, and even among them, not all had it in for Jesus. Still, the Jews as a whole have always been one of the easiest targets of hatred for Christians; that was true in the medieval period, and it's true in the modern period.

Charles Coughlin was the Rush Limbaugh of his day. A popular 1930s US talk radio personality and Catholic priest, he "told it like it was," and millions of listeners ate it up. Early in his radio career, he helped Franklin D. Roosevelt by heavily promoting the New Deal on his show. By all accounts, he was probably the most influential Catholic of his day. He even pulled an Alec Baldwin[1] by promising voters he would leave broadcasting if William Lemke[2] wasn't elected president. Most of you readers are probably saying, "Who the heck is William Lemke?" which should tell you that he obviously was not elected. Coughlin did leave—but only for a short time.

Coughlin also had a giant man-crush on Adolf Hitler. You read that right: a man whom millions of people looked to as a moral leader loved a murderous dictator. How did that happen? Easy: like Hitler, Coughlin hated Jews. *Really* hated them. Coughlin had no problem blaming most of the country's woes leading up to World War II on those pesky Jewish bankers.

---

1. Who famously said he would leave the United States if Bush was elected.
2. Congressman Lemke was the Union Party's presidential candidate in 1936. He failed to get even 2 percent of the vote.

When he realized the error of his ways, he tried to distance him-self from anti-Semitism. He went as far as saying he wanted to help Jewish people. But then he went on to support the Christian Front.[3]

By the 1940s, the government decided that in time of war, it wasn't in the country's best interests to let a guy who was sort of pro-Hitler stay on the air and influence Americans. In the end, Coughlin's bishop, Edward Mooney, ordered Coughlin to essen-tially shut up and get back to being a priest. If he didn't, he would be defrocked. Coughlin obeyed and died in relative obscurity in 1979.

It's hard to read this story and not wonder how a Christian—a priest, no less—could get so riled up, to the point of spewing out hateful messages to millions of listeners. But that's what power does in the hearts of many Christians: it makes us forget what we're called here to do.

Sun Myung Moon spent much of his early life in North Korean labor camps. The experience made him anti-Communist. It also helped instill a strong family values message in his ministry. In 1954, Moon founded the Unification Church in Seoul. Moon was raised a Protestant, and in the beginnings that was clear. But as Moon's church got more and more popular, his doctrine began to evolve, and at his ministry's height, Moon announced that he was the Messiah.

It was bad enough for a man with such a strong Christian back-ground to believe he was the Messiah, but Moon had a hankering to make things worse by telling his millions of followers that Jews had the whole holocaust thing coming because they killed Jesus.

Why all the hate? Easy—it's biblical. Jesus says in Matthew 10:34, "Do not suppose that I have come to bring peace to the earth. I did not come to bring peace, but a sword." So there you have it: Jesus himself has given us a call to arms! Let's get locked and loaded, cowboy!

---

3. An organization started because of Coughlin, whose core mission was to make people aware of those pesky Jewish bankers.

Except that's not what this verse is about, so simmer down. Christ was saying that happy times are not here. He was not coming to end all violence; rather, he was warning his disciples that they had entered into a new age of persecution. And indeed, his words came true. Thousands and thousands of Christians were slaughtered, and even today Christians continue to be martyred for their belief.

The sword was not a literal sword. Otherwise, when Peter cut the ear of the Roman soldier,[4] Jesus would have high-fived him. Instead, Jesus rebuked Peter.

The sword was a spiritual sword. Christ was saying that Christians needed—and need—to be prepared for persecution. We need to arm ourselves spiritually. The time to build ourselves up isn't when the attack is under way; we have to be ready for the violence that is going to come to us. We must be on guard spiritually at all times.

That means Christians shouldn't give unbelievers reasons to attack them. We can't live a life that leads people to smirk and say, "Figures they're a Christian, because they're a horrible person."

That's what the sword means. But as soon as Christians gained the upper hand in Europe, there was a reversal of rules. Christians gained political clout and began forcing their belief on others. Once you were conquered, suddenly you were a Christian. Congratulations.

Jews were a fun target for many Christians for the first few centuries, but these Christians have evolved a lot since then. Today those Christians are much kinder about sharing the love by hating people of all creeds and cultures.

The Lord's Resistance Army (LRA) has carried out all the marks of evil. Murders. Raping women. Forcing women to become wives to soldiers, who then give their wives the gift of AIDS. Forcing children into the army. All in the name of Jesus.

It is all too easy to say that this is just an extremist group that took Christ's so-called call to arms too literally. But that's the thing: there are only two ways to take it. You believe either that Christ meant a

---

4. This is in all four gospels, so clearly Christians of the early church thought it was important (see Matt. 26:51; Mark 14:47; Luke 22:50; John 18:10).

spiritual sword, or that he meant a literal one. And if you believe he meant a literal one, then guess what? The LRA is what you get.

People, for the most part, are much more civil and tolerable than they were hundreds of years ago, and that can be problematic for Jesus's call to arms. Since it's not very politically correct to say the sword is physical, some have taken it to a whole new level by saying the sword is neither physical nor spiritual—it's apocryphal. This means that the verse is a reference to a time in the future when Christians will be at war, when unbelievers will have the mark of the Beast, and when believers will have to fight.

Funny thing about this theory of Christian warfare. The Bible says that for us "to live is Christ and to die is gain" (Phil. 1:21). What does that mean? For starters, we go to heaven! And if we believe that, then we have to ask ourselves why we are fighting with the sword. Why would we want to extend our life? We get paradise!

Here's the thing about heaven: there's plenty of room. God doesn't need you to fight with the sword to protect yourself or his kingdom. If you believe in God and you die in some apocryphal horror house, then you get to go to heaven. Your mission on earth is to help God's kingdom spread. You'll never be able to do that with a literal sword in hand, or any weapon.

Wiki Break

It's unfortunate that Christianity, which should be one of the most loving religions, has a long history of hate. The most famous example? The Crusades. Below is a quick recap.

In 1095, the Byzantine emperor requested the volunteer aid of Pope Urban II to help fight off the Turks.[5] The Pope sent aid but soon attached an additional goal: take back the Holy Land.

---

5. The Turks established a reputation of treating Christian pilgrims a little harshly.

What started as a request for volunteer aid ended with what would become known as the Crusades. It spanned over a hundred years, and millions died, making it one of the deadliest wars ever fought—all in the name of Christ. Think the LRA is extreme? Their war crimes are nothing next to the acts committed in the Crusades.

How bloody were the Crusades? All war is bloody, but here are two fun facts:

1. In 1098, during the siege of Ma'arra, Raymond de Saint Gilles led his men to a victorious siege. Thousands were slaughtered. Gilles's soldiers partied like it was 1999—until they realized there was no food. Then they started eating people.

2. Richard the Lionhearted, king of England, notoriously had some three thousand Muslim prisoners executed, including women and children. Why did he do it? According to legend, he had originally told Muslim leaders that if they gave him the True Cross on which Christ was crucified, then he would hand over his prisoners. When they didn't hand over the cross, he let them watch as he had each of the three thousand killed. If that isn't a total misunderstanding of what the cross represents, then I don't know what is.

The Crusades were started to protect Christendom against Muslims. In all fairness, there was a threat, and strategically, providing such protection may have been the best thing to do. But Christianity isn't about strategy. In the end, God isn't going to say it was good that you slaughtered thousands of people because they *could have* invaded your territory. One can only guess what would have happened during the Crusades if Christians had acted a little more Christianly.

When you walk with a literal sword, you are saying you choose to play God—to have the ability to take life. You aren't saying you believe that God can and will protect you. You don't need a sword to receive God's protection. You only need one thing: God.

A lot of people believe in Christianity because they view it as good for networking or simply fun. But Christianity isn't fun. Driving your car five miles over the speed limit is fun. Visiting a bizarre and obscure museum is fun.[6] Christianity—not fun.

My money is on the disciples having a spirited ministry with lots of good laughs. But no Christians were laughing on the way to their martyrdom. It's okay to laugh, to goof around. That's natural. The trouble is, sometimes we put so much emphasis on enjoying life that we forget what we were called to do.

I've seen churches with gun ministries. If you want to own a gun, own a gun. But when we start attaching ministry to it, then we might be missing something. The emphasis of so-called gun ministries revolves around using guns as a form of leadership: intense, manly training whereby one learns important, Christ-centered values such as outdoor survival, guerrilla combat, and how to spot the mark of the Beast.

Christians aren't all violent, of course. But violence is only one form of hate. In God's eyes, holding a grudge against someone or simply not loving them is the exact same thing as murdering them.

The thing about sin is, it's sin. James 2:10 says, "Whoever keeps the whole law and yet stumbles at just one point is guilty of breaking all of it." And further, 1 John 3:15 says, "Everyone who hates his brother is a murderer; and you know that no murderer has eternal life abiding in him" (NASB). There's no such thing as the greater sin. In man's eyes, there are worse evils, but in the eyes of God, evil is sin and no sin is greater. When you hate another person you are committing the same sin as murdering that person—because sin is sin. Christ redeems us from our sins, but you're kidding yourself if you think you can continue hating because there are worse sins. There are no "worse sins."

When bad things happen, we have an instinct to fight back. Nobody is surprised when a father gets revenge on the man who

---

6. I'm looking at you, Vent Haven: Ventriloquist Museum—open May through September!

murdered his wife or child. Why wouldn't he want revenge? It's a natural feeling. But Christianity is about living outside of those natural feelings and impulses. It's about mercy, about not giving people what they rightly deserve.

Christ hasn't called us to be like humanity; Christ has called us to be like him. The hardest part of Christianity is living in a way that is unexpected. Becoming Christlike is not comfortable. It calls us out of our comfort zones to a place where our first thought isn't "How can I get revenge?" It's "How can I love them anyway?"

Grace is the most amazing gift God gave us to offer others. It's the ability to do something extraordinary and completely unnatural: to love where we have no reason to love. That is a powerful thing. That kind of power can change the world.

But while Christians affirm that through grace Christ died for us, accepting this gift from God and doing the same toward others is a gift Christians would rather return. And I wouldn't blame anyone for wanting a refund! On paper, that kind of grace sounds really bad. But in practice, something out of this world happens: we feel God's presence. We feel close to God.

Go ahead, try it. I'm not talking about giving a dollar to a homeless man;[7] what I'm talking about is going to the person who hates you most—whoever it is—and doing something they wouldn't expect: love them.

If you are living your life as a Christian and everything feels well and good, then perhaps you are doing something wrong. Growth

---

7. I'm not saying you shouldn't do that, though—you should. Don't take the "He's just going to spend it on beer" or "I saw on the news a person who makes $500 a day panhandling on the corner" card, because only God knows what that person's situation is.

comes when we have growing pains, when we feel ourselves being stretched and pulled.

When Jesus turned over the tables of the money changers in the Jerusalem temple, he wasn't angry at the Romans, and he wasn't rising up in fury against the unbelievers. He was mad at his own people. He was holding them accountable for their absolute disgrace of the temple.

What would happen if, instead of directing our anger at non-Christians, we Christians took our own kind to task? It's not the unbelievers who need to be shaken up and awakened, it's the believers. For all the talk about the need for spiritual revival in the world, revival starts in the church when people get a little uncomfortable. It starts when people submit completely to God—when they surrender and say, "God, it's not about how I feel and what I want; it's about how I can live my life to serve you." That certainly applies to our impulse to repay violence with more violence. Hate has never solved a conflict. Hate only gives birth to more hate.

The unfortunate truth about the family we were born into when we were born again is it's abusive. And those born into an abusive family are likely to repeat the cycle of abuse. Cycles are easier to repeat than change. But the cycle can be broken. The abuse can stop. The chain can be broken.

When asked what the greatest commandment was, Christ answered, "'Love the Lord your God with all your heart and with all your soul and with all your mind.' This is the first and greatest commandment. And the second is like it: 'Love your neighbor as yourself.' All the Law and the Prophets hang on these two commandments" (Matt. 22:37–40). It should be no shock that loving our neighbor is the greatest commandment next to loving God. Loving our neighbor sums up Christianity. The Bible doesn't provide a contingency plan; it doesn't tell us to love our neighbor but carry a sword just in case.

We have to be on guard always. We have to be ready to fight. But the fight isn't against those who try to harm us physically—it's against those who try to harm us spiritually. You can't fight a spiritual battle with a physical sword.

If you are looking for your mission, then that's it: Love your neighbor. If even a fourth of all Christians did this, then a spiritual revolution would begin.

Getting Social

Twitter: Tweet what grace means to you: #JesusLoves.

Pinterest: Create a board called "Jesus Loves" that's full of articles and pictures of Christians doing extraordinary things.

Instagram: Take and share a picture that captures this love: #JesusLoves.

LinkedIn: Add "hugger" as a job skill. Bonus points: Hug anyone who endorses your skill.

Facebook: Write a post about what grace means to you.

Which Bible Hero Are You?

What would you do if someone gave you a million dollars and told you to do with it as you pleased?

- A. Retire into solitude (+1)
- B. Use it to help people (+3)
- C. Give it to my family (+5)
- D. Start a business (+7)
- E. Use it to pay for my brilliant invention (+9)
- F. Do something utterly ridiculous (+11)

Christian Hard Rock

#RockingTheHymnal

SHARE

Basketball Team   **A-Team**   **Praise Team**

It starts normally. Innocently. A pleasant church, friendly people. But then the hands come up. The *Praise Jesus*es start. And suddenly, not having the same emotional reaction to the music makes you . . . different.

Being moved by the Spirit during a song is by no means a false reaction. It is a valid way to experience the Spirit of God. Not only is it valid, but it's common. I wouldn't be far off to suggest it might be the most popular way to feel the presence of God.

But it's not the only way. That funky, guitar-strumming, drum-banging praise music you hear in nearly every church is a relatively new phenomenon. While praise music is most popularly seen in evangelical churches, its origins can be largely traced to a reformed Christian monk[1] in the 1950s in France.

---

1. Otherwise known as "a Calvinist."

Roger Schütz (known by most as Brother Roger) left his native Switzerland in 1940 because it wasn't much affected by World War II. He wanted to go where people were hurting and suffering, and he picked France—Taizé, Saône-et-Loire, to be more precise. In the early days, he used his ministry, in part, to hide Jewish refugees, but he was ultimately forced out by the Nazis. He returned in 1944 and, under his humble guidance, the Taizé Community began to grow. The Community was unusual in that it reached across all Christian divisions, becoming a home to Protestant and Catholic monks alike.

In the 1960s, the Community really began taking off. In keeping with Brother Roger's heart for youth, it held meetings for young adults from all more than the world. The first such meeting had 1,400 people from over twenty-five countries. Under Brother Roger's leadership, music became one of the ways to engage the visitors. To this day, over five thousand students visit the Community each summer. The typical meeting is just prayer and music.

Brother Roger died at the age of ninety when a mentally ill woman stabbed him during a prayer service. His funeral was presided over by a Catholic cardinal, which is pretty darn rare. Yet as far-reaching as his impact has been, you've probably never heard of Brother Roger until now, because he rarely gave interviews and did everything possible to keep a low profile.

When you go to church, consider that all the hand-raising praise is due in part to a little-known monk in France who tried to encourage devotion and worship across all communities of Christianity.

I was in my mid-teens when I saw it—an arm-raising, "Yes, Jesus," praising person. He was teary-eyed by the time the guitar strumming worship leader finished his tune. During his encore performance, more people raised their hands in praise until, finally, I did too. But I didn't feel the Spirit of God. I felt the spirit of peer pressure—the spirit of wandering eyes which, I felt certain, would judge me if I didn't feel the presence of God.

Raising my hands in unauthentic praise taught me something valuable: it's not hard to imitate worship. Just take a deep breath, get a little relaxed, and raise up your hands. For good measure, throw in a sensual moan or two.

When I was young, there was no such thing as a worship team. There was the choir, but that was it. I grew up in a more traditional environment. Yet music was a big part of my upbringing. My grandma was a church organist; that's what I remember most about her and the thing she was proudest of.

She was a go-to organist in Orange County, and she proudly told me several times how she had played the organ on one occasion at the Los Angeles Memorial Sports Arena.[2] She was also the piano teacher of choice for hundreds of pianists in the making.

Grandma no doubt felt God's presence when she played. She probably knew more hymns than Bible verses, and I'm sure God was okay with that. She made music an important part of her grandkids' childhood and tried to get my brother and me to play. (We didn't, of course.) My grandmother represented what I knew about worship—which is to say, hymns sung with little fanfare.

When I finally heard church music plugged into an amplifier, it was a welcome sound next to the ritualistic, stiff-sounding pew music I was used to. It gave a bit of energy to the service and was no doubt sincere. But it was still just a sound.

If the praise-type worship we know today is a relatively recent phenomenon, then what did worship look like for the early church?

The New Testament gives us plenty of examples, and they're mostly what you might think of as a home Bible study, because the

---

2. Former home to the Los Angeles Clippers.

early church was more community oriented. But outside of the Bible we also have plenty of other examples. One of the best is given by Justin Martyr.[3] According to his *First Apology*,[4] written in AD 155, church went down as follows . . .

First, the "memoirs of the apostles or the writings of the prophets are read."[5] Next, a minister (or "president" as Justin referred to him) would get up and urge people to imitate what was in the reading. Then they'd all stand up and pray. After prayer, they'd take communion and pray once more, and the people who "prospered" or wanted to contribute would give an offering to help take care of orphans, widows, and the sick.

Sound familiar? It should, because that's essentially the same formula churches have followed for centuries.[6]

Ever wonder why church is on Sunday and not on Saturday, when observant Jews worship? Justin explains that too: it's because Sunday is when Christ rose from the dead. You can, of course, go to church any day you want; but for the early church, when people actually did have the same day off, it was all but expected that you would make Sunday the day to go to church.

What did the early church think of praise music—or rather, of using instruments in music? Not too highly. Thomas Aquinas, one of the greatest thinkers of Christian philosophy, said his church didn't want to use musical instruments because it may seem like they were trying to "Judaize." The great theologian Augustine of Hippo, who wrote two of the most studied works in Christianity,[7] said instru-

---

3. If you want to know who he is, then stayed tuned for the Wiki Break.
4. When we say "apology" today, it means we're basically asking forgiveness for something we did; here, however, *apology* refers to the defense of a position. So *First Apology* should be read as his first argument for belief in Christianity.
5. Justin Martyr, ch. 67, "Weekly Worship of the Christians," in *First Apology*. "Memoirs of the apostles" are most likely the Gospels.
6. If it doesn't sound familiar because your church meetings consist of two hours of drinking snake venom and smearing goat's blood on yourselves, then your church might have a problem—and it probably isn't as Christian as you first thought.
7. *City of God* and *Confessions*.

ments shouldn't be used because they made church seem like a theater or circus. Erasmus, nicknamed "Prince of the Humanists,"[8] said essentially the same thing as Augustine. John Calvin wasn't fond of instrumental music because the Catholics got the idea for it from the Jews. Even good old John Wesley, whose brother, Charles Wesley,[9] wrote over six thousand hymns,[10] said musical instruments should not be seen or heard.

For these great thinkers, the only instruments needed were our voices. They weren't worried so much about the sound (though some were); usually they were concerned about the way churches would use instruments to make things a little more . . . secular. They worried that the church would become just a place to go for entertainment and that people wouldn't grow closer to God but would just feel good about themselves.

WikiBreak

Justin Martyr was born into a pagan family in 100 BC. He was well versed in classical philosophers like Socrates and Plato. He firmly believed the arguments and philosophical teachings of Plato—until one day he met a Christian, who taught him a new kind of philosophy, and Justin became a believer.

He became perhaps the greatest apologist of the early church. He started some of the first schools of Christian thought and helped form theological foundations that would eventually go into pretty much every church.

Philippians 1:21 says that "to live is Christ and to die is gain." Justin took those words to heart, as did many early Christians. Justin knew the climate of the empire and fully expected to be persecuted. And he was. Unlike the martyrdom of some, which some scholars

---

8. Humanists of Erasmus's time emphasized the human nature of Jesus and his social teachings.
9. While his big brother, John Wesley, gets all the attention for starting the Methodist movement, Charles Wesley was great in his own right.
10. Many, like "Hark! The Herald Angels Sing," are still sung today.

say never happened, Justin's is well documented. Brought to trial and ordered to sacrifice to other gods or face torture, he replied, bluntly, that he would rather face the torture of some Roman nut job than the torture of God. Death, Justin fully believed, meant salvation. He was beheaded with several other Christians.

I'm the opposite of most people; it's incredibly rare for me to be truly moved by a song. For me, writing is worship; it's when I'm writing that I really feel the presence of God. I feel like I'm doing something I would not otherwise be able to do. I feel pleasure. I feel closeness to God. If I ever doubt God, picking up a paper and pen erases all uncertainty.

Worship comes in many forms and is different for every person.

There's absolutely nothing wrong with worship music, of course; the fact that music does little for me doesn't make it any less valid. But it doesn't last. Praise music may put you in a good mood, give you a spiritual high of sorts, but that high goes away rather quickly. A car cuts you off as you're leaving the parking lot, and like that, the high is gone.

The danger of worship music is that people start relying on it. They go to church so they can have their weekly dose of feeling God. That gets them through their week. Nothing wrong with that, except for one thing: we shouldn't rely on a weekly experience, and one that's only an hour long at that.[11] Church is where we go to fellowship with like-minded believers. But fellowship isn't the only component of worship. We need to be able to worship God in all moments. Anyone can go to church and call it a day.

WikiBreak

Modern worship may not have a lot of history, but church music in general goes back a long way. The Psalms are, of course, some of the

---

11. Or maybe up to two hours, if you go to a church that is extra devoted.

earliest examples of hymns. The New Testament says several times that believers would sing hymns.[12]

The Lutheran church is responsible for providing thousands of hymns. Charles Wesley, one of the greatest hymn writers who ever lived, helped spread the message of the Methodist church through the hymns he wrote.

The first significant shift between traditional hymn music and modern Christian music was with the introduction of gospel music. While we may think of gospel as something that originated in the African community, gospel "hymns" were perfected by a less likely culprit: a white guy. In the nineteenth century, with revival riding high in America, the evangelist Dwight L. Moody partnered with vocalist and composer Ira D. Sankey to create music that working-class people could relate to.

There's a dirty secret to worship: it can be made up. An atheist can make good worship music. You don't need to be a Christian to make inspiring, Holy Spirit–feeling music. An atheist can imitate the sound of worship to the same effect. It is not at all a rare occurrence for a "Christian band" that has toured under the banner of Christianity to distance itself from the faith that made them money, and even admit they weren't really Christians after all. Saying you're a Christian can earn you solid cash in entertainment, so a lot of performers figure, why not?

There are often two facades of the Christian church: the one you see onstage and the one you don't see backstage. One can only hope to attend a church with the same backstage as front stage, but let's be honest: churches aren't always honest. Backstage things happen. The sincerity you witness onstage may not be sincere. There is lying, cheating, even stealing. You'd never know it from the music being played—from the smiles on a leader's face, the joy in his voice, the tears in his prayers. But those things don't mean he's for real.

---

12. See Matthew 26:30; 1 Corinthians 14:26; Ephesians 5:19; Colossians 3:16.

And that suggests a very important question: How do we know what's authentic and what just feels good? That the person onstage isn't leading us to experience something based on fakery? How do we know the church we attend has the same background and foreground?

And how do we know that the feelings we may experience are even real—that they are more than just feelings, that they are authentic, that the Spirit is truly moving us? It's said that you can't see God, but you can feel him—but how do we know that what we are feeling is God?

We live life in a ritualistic way. We wake up at a set time, go to work at a set time, take our lunch at a set time, come home at a set time, and go to bed at a set time. Our entire life is formed around the idea that things need to be scheduled. The reason worship throughout the week doesn't work for so many people is that God doesn't work on a schedule. You can say, "God, I'm giving you five o'clock." But God works best when you allow him spontaneity.

Do you follow Christ in every moment, or do you follow him when you feel guilty about something? Do you look for ways to worship God, or do you wait until God comes knocking and asks you to do something? Because if you are waiting for God to come to you, then you probably are missing the whole point of worship.

Worshiping God is anything that opens your eyes to him. It's anything that makes you feel his presence. You don't have to sing a song for that.

If you limit God's day to church day, then you have a problem. Fortunately, God's day isn't limited. It's every day, all the time. This moment. This second. This is God's. You are God's.

Worship begins to happen the moment we realize we are dead. That right now we are not alive. That God lives through us in everything we do. God. Everything. We live to serve God.

When was the last time you told God that your life is his to use? God is your master, you are his servant, and your only role in this life is to expand his kingdom. Anything you do to spread the kingdom of God is worship.

When we ask how to worship God, maybe we're asking the wrong question. Maybe we should be asking, How can I make God's kingdom greater? We each have gifts that equip us to do so—physical gifts and spiritual gifts. This world operates because God has uniquely gifted each of us to help make the world go round. A vast majority of us recognize our talents and use them—but for our own gain. We're good at business, for instance, so we start a business, but that business is separate from God's business. However, when we combine our physical gifts with our spiritual gifts, the world both within us and around us begins to transform.

That's how we know that worship is authentic and not just a feeling: because when we truly worship God, we experience inner transformation. Our old self is dead and in its place is a new person.

The legacy we create is another case in point. Typically it has more to do with our children than God's children. It's about leaving something behind for the family, whether it's a house or money. But what if we started thinking about legacy differently? What if we considered how our legacy can make God's kingdom larger?

We tend to make worship about the things we can see and hear. It's easy to get emotionally invested in a song, because we can hear the words and the music, we can see others being moved, and we are moved likewise. But worship that lasts is worship that can't be seen or heard, it can only be felt. Worship that happens when it's quiet, that happens when you surrender yourself to God and ask him to let you be a vessel committed to making this world God's kingdom. Worship that happens when you combine your physical and your spiritual gifts.

Early Christians didn't have the wealth of the world. Today we have lots of distractions that make it difficult to worship God. Sometimes we just have to turn it all off and make God the focus. When we look through a blurry lens, naturally we complain that we can't see anything. But focus the lens and things suddenly become clearer. To worship God, sometimes we just need a new pair of glasses to give us a new or renewed perspective on life.

If you want worship to last, you have to take time to personally experience it. If lifting your hands, inspired by the worship music others have created, makes you feel close to God, then great! But if you aren't seeking out other forms of worship as well, then you are missing out.

Getting Social

Turn it off. All of it. Get social . . . with God.

Chapter Twelve

What the Faith!

#F8ful

The rapture isn't biblical.[1] Not entirely, anyway. It's not even historical. It's a relatively recent phenomenon.

Fans of the rapture will, of course, point to Revelation when referencing its events, but they are wrong. They aren't even in the right century. If you want to learn about the rapture, then you need to wait until the Puritan movement of the eighteenth century. Prior to that, the concept was around but not popular.

The second-coming theology that is widely believed today was actually created by Cotton Mather.[2] A few years after Mather's death, a now-forgotten theologian named Philip Doddridge used

---

1. The rapture is the idea that Christians will be caught up to heaven while nonbelievers are left behind during the final days of earth.
2. The same puritanical nut whom most scholars credit with laying the groundwork for the Salem witch trials.

the word *rapture* as a theological term in a Bible commentary. But even after that, the rapture wasn't a big deal. Not until the Cold War came along and got everyone worried about the end of the world did it really catch on. Now it's huge.

A few years ago, a little book made big waves in the Christian marketplace. It was called *Left Behind*. It spawned movies,[3] spin-off books for kids, and even a video game.[4] And it got a lot of people talking about the so-called end times. Hundreds of books on the subject were published; people just couldn't get enough of it. Churches even started making kits to help the people who would be left behind.

The topic was nothing new, of course, but the book put a fresh spin on the rapture and renewed interest in the topic. While the word *rapture* is not in the Bible, Mather and Doddridge weren't just making things up. The Bible laid the foundation for it. The reason it never took off was because the theology was a bit radical. Up to this point, most Christians believed that believers would be taken up to heaven when Jesus returned, but there would be no people left behind. The Cold War, however, made the world feel a bit doomsdayish, and the theory really began to gather steam, especially with evangelicals.

Christians universally accept that there will be an end time called the tribulation; most agree that the period is seven years,[5] and then Jesus will come and take believers to heaven. It's the whole rapture thing that becomes fuzzy theology. Today there are five popular views on the rapture:

- Pretribulation: The rapture will come prior to the seven years of tribulation, but the actual second coming of Christ won't happen until the end of the seven years.

---

3. One with Kirk Cameron (hint: it's not *Growing Pains: Return of the Seavers*) and one with Nicolas Cage.
4. It was sort of the Christian equivalent of *Grand Theft Auto*. Believers had to try to convert unbelievers, and when necessary, kill them—all in the name of Jesus, of course. It spawned three sequels.
5. Though even that is debatable.

- Midtribulation: The rapture will come in the middle of the tribulation period.
- Prewrath: The rapture will happen at some point during the tribulation period.
- Partial Rapture: Some Christians will be raptured before the tribulation, but others will endure the seven-year tribulation before they get raptured.[6]
- Posttribulation: Christians will be raptured at the end of the seven years of tribulation.

All the theology points to a reality, but that doesn't mean we should worry about it. End-time theology isn't about us; the Bible tells us to live for the moment, not for the past or the future.[7]

What does all this mean? In short: Christianity is weird. Really. Messy, actually. Christian faith? Not so much.

If things got no messier than rapture theology, we might not be so bad off. But the mess is everywhere.

Think about angels. Aw . . . *angels!* Just the thought of them brings warm fuzzies to your soul. How could you not like angels? They're there for you. Protecting you. Pulling you out of danger.

Angel theology is popular. Movies are made about angels. There's this idea that all of us have a little guardian angel watching over us. But none of it is biblical.

The Bible does say plenty about angels; there are nearly three hundred unique references to them. But their role is most often that of a messenger or a minister to humans. God certainly uses angels to help humans, but to say we have one assigned to us is a bit of a stretch. The danger of angel theology is, it's gotten to the point where people are in a near-worship state. They'd much rather think about angels than God.

---

6. Though some say it won't actually be at the end.
7. Matthew 6:34.

Just as angels are often misunderstood, so is satan. The popular image of a red guy with horns and a pitchfork is not taken from the Bible. The Bible doesn't say as much about satan as you would think. Ezekiel 28:12–18 describes him as someone who was created quite beautiful—he had the seal of perfection and was full of wisdom. But pride got the best of him, and he turned on God. He became a tempter and deceiver to humankind.

When did he get his horns? It's widely agreed that Christians derived their images of satan from the Roman gods, particularly the horned god named Pan. As for the Bible, Ezekiel 28:14 calls him a cherub, and chapters 1 and 10 of Ezekiel describe the cherubim as fantastic winged creatures. Chapter 28 further portrays satan in its description of the king of Tyre, whom theologians widely agree is a type of satan. It's safe to say that satan is a far more mind-boggling and terrifying being than the cartoon figure people often think of.

To add insult to injury, one only needs to turn to the past two hundred-some-odd years of history to see how a messy Christianity has gotten in the way of just about everything. When there's a controversial issue at hand, you can almost certainly count on a few Christians springing into action to help crush it down, even if the Bible says nothing on the subject. Here are a few examples:

- Slavery: The Bible letter of Philemon is about as antislavery as you can get. There were slaves in the Bible, but the Bible is more about letting slaves go. So how is it that slave owners claimed to be Christian? With verses like these: "Slaves, obey your earthly masters with fear and trembling" (Eph. 6:5 NRSV), and "Tell slaves to be submissive to their masters and to give satisfaction in every respect" (Titus 2:9 NRSV).

  Pretty convincing stuff—if only it wasn't taken out of context. In the case of Ephesians, the very next verse tells slaves why they should obey: "Not only to win their [master's] favor when their eye is on you, but as slaves of Christ, doing the will of God from your heart" (Eph. 6:6). Then it goes on to address slave owners: "Masters, treat your slaves in the same way. Do not threaten them, since you know that he who is both their Master and yours is in heaven, and there is no favoritism with him" (Eph. 6:9). The goal is to bring believers to equality.

In the case of Titus, the chapter goes on to explain that the goal was to bring the master to Christ. He would then become a brother in Christ to the slave! The end game for all the Bible writers was not to have slavery, but to have a system of family in which everyone worked together and was equal.

- Segregation: It's all well and good to say we shouldn't bind up a person and treat them as our property, but should we *really* say that all race is the same? Hopefully, today that's a no-brainer yes for you. But historically, what did Christians say about the subject?

  To be fair, many were huge supporters of abolishing both slavery and segregation. Still, some groups used the Bible to support their segregation efforts. Since the New Testament didn't back them up, they twisted its interpretation; for the most part, though, they referred to the Old Testament. But there were two problems with that approach. First, the Old Testament law went away with the cross of Christ;[8] and second, the segregation referenced in the Old Testament was about preserving purity of religion, not race; its intent was to stop Jewish believers from marrying outsiders who would corrupt their faith with pagan rituals. Acts 10:28 gives perhaps the best rationale about why this is no longer applicable: "You are well aware that it is against our law for a Jew to associate with or visit a Gentile. But God has shown me that I should not call anyone impure or unclean."

---

8. At least if you are a Christian.

- Women's Suffrage: Today the idea of a woman's being able to vote and work just makes sense. But little more than a hundred years ago, some Christians saw this as the biggest threat not just to society but also to the Christian faith.

   The Bible, of course, was their defense. For instance, 1 Corinthians 14:35 says, "It is disgraceful for a woman to speak in the church," and 1 Timothy 2:11–12 says, "A woman should learn in quietness and full submission. I do not permit a woman to teach or to assume authority over a man; she must be quiet." For two thousand years these verses were widely interpreted as, "Shut up, woman."

   When people use the Bible as their defense, they typically do so in a talk radio sort of way—lots of angry screaming, with no pausing to understand what Scripture really does teach. At face value, both of the above verses make women seem like lesser beings next to men, which of course is not true. In both cases scholars agree that, taken in context, the verses came about because women were abusing spiritual gifts and creating chaos in the church. The role a woman should play in church is more debatable. But it has absolutely nothing to do with her role in society.

- Contraceptives: Condoms have been around for more than four hundred years. The first were made out of intestines and bladders; it wasn't until the eighteenth century that condom sales really took off, but it was more of an upper-class thing because they were so expensive.

   This all changed thanks to Charles Goodyear and the marvelous invention of rubber. But as with all things new, Christians took note and then took to the Bible. Even today, some will argue that contraceptives are not only bad but unbiblical, and they will point to one of the Bible's most misinterpreted stories: the story of Onan (Gen. 38). For those not familiar with the NSFW (Not Safe For Work) account, it goes like this: Judah had two sons: Er and Onan. Er married a fine lady named Tamar, but he did wicked things and died before Tamar had children.

According to the law at the time, Onan had to marry Tamar. But Onan didn't want to give Tamar any children; he saw that as producing on his brother's behalf, and he didn't want to give Er the satisfaction.[9] So Onan had sex with Tamar, but he pulled out before finishing the deed. So God put Onan to death.

This story has nothing to do with birth control. To say so misses the point of the story, namely, that Onan refused to fulfill his legal obligation to create an heir for his dead brother. So what *does* the Bible say about contraception? Not a whole lot. It says plenty on children and the blessing they are, but it never condemns those who decide not to have children.

USELESS POLL

The end of the world is . . .

A. near.
B. an idea some people use to strike fear in others.
C. here.
D. something that will happen, but why dwell on it?

To be part of this poll, visit:
www.OrganicJesus.com/useless-polls

- Prohibition: How can a Christian say drinking is wrong when Jesus himself turned water to wine and drank with his disciples? Yet, of the many things Christians have gotten wrong over the years, prohibition is one they didn't get completely wrong.

  As with many things, prohibition was extreme. However, it wasn't so much about drinking as drunkenness, and drunkenness is something the Bible frowns upon.[10] The problem, of course, is Christians cannot dictate the behaviors of others. And they certainly can't forbid people to do something that the Bible not only says is okay, but, in the case of fermented drink, is actually used for some of its rituals.

---

9. Nothing like a little brotherly unlove.
10. See Ephesians 5:18.

Jesus Christ makes sense when we look at him from a purely organic standpoint. The problem with Christianity isn't the Christ part—it's the "ianity" part. Insert the letters "ns" there, and what do you get? Insanity.

And that's just it—over the past two thousand-some years, we've added all this stuff to it. All these years have given us way too much time to think, and so we've added all these rituals, rites, and sacraments. Some may be important; others, not so much. But the result is that being a Christian today doesn't look very different from being a Jew three thousand years ago. There are codes to follow. We don't call them laws, but we sure know how to judge you for not following our not-laws.

But Christ got rid of all those pesky Jewish laws. You know all those weird Old Testament commandments that told women what to do during their period and men how to respond to diarrhea? Well, Christ came and swept all that away. And he didn't do it so we could replace it with another system of dos and don'ts. The only thing we need to worry about is believing in him. That makes sense. Easy theology.

WikiBreak

There was more division in the early church than we are sometimes led to believe. And why wouldn't there be? Jesus came and did all those fancy miracles, so it makes sense that stories would quickly spread—so much so that he became a bit of a folk icon. Gnosticism was born out of these legends.

The introduction to the gospel of Luke (1:1–4) may in some ways point to where Gnosticism began. Luke writes about the many accounts circulating and implies that he is writing his gospel so that people will have the best historical record.

Gnostics believed they possessed a secret knowledge of God, which is how they made sense of some of their more unorthodox theology.

Sometimes their beliefs fit the mainstream; other times, they were way out of whack. The wave of Gnostics was loudest in the second and third centuries and largely fizzled out by the fourth, though you can still find it even today. There were hundreds of different branches, and they all believed different things. Among the weird highlights:

- Abelians were required to marry, but they couldn't consummate the marriage. Since they needed kids to keep the religion alive, they were required to adopt a boy and a girl.
- Manichaeism taught that its founder was the reincarnation of several people—notably Jesus, Buddha, and Krishna.
- The Bardaisanite sect believed that the sun, moon, and all other planets were living beings.
- During several of their rituals, the Borborites would smear their hands with menstrual blood and semen. Many of their rituals include intercourse—but not to worry: if a woman got pregnant, they would eat the fetus.

When people bring up all the apocryphal books of the New Testament that the church is supposedly hiding from believers, they are referring mostly to books that Gnostic groups wrote to help explain their beliefs.

It is painful to think about how many people have outright abandoned Christ not because they didn't believe in him, but because they didn't believe in the church.

If you're a new Christian, things usually go well—at first. You accept Christ. You go to Bible studies. You sing songs and raise your hands in praise. You feel the Holy Spirit. You feel good.

But then someone wrongs you—or worse, someone tells you that you aren't being very Christian. And that's usually the moment when the dark side of the church starts crashing in. We all need to be accountable; what's bothersome is the way that people hold others accountable. Some people say they can't get married because one person is Catholic and the other is Protestant. I've been to funerals where I can't take communion because I don't subscribe to a certain doctrine of that particular church.

When theology gets messy, the church gets messy.

How many people would be saved if we got back to the simple truth of the gospel: Jesus saves. That's all that matters. I'm different from you; God calls me to live a certain way. My path to return to God is different from yours. I love theology. I love studying it and learning how Christianity was shaped. I feel closer to God when I delve into it; my mind gets opened in amazing ways. But if I told Diana to get dressed up, took her somewhere nice, and then said, "Tonight I want to talk about Dynamic Monarchianism," she would not be too happy. Because her path is different. I can't tell her how to live her life or get close to God. If she is doing something that is bringing her away from God, then I can certainly tell her to stop it. But a better way would be to let God tell her. If I can help her connect with him, then he can redeem her soul through the Spirit and not through condemnation.

In Luke 15:11–32, Jesus tells one of his best-known parables: the parable of the lost son.[11] People turn to it as a teaching on forgiveness, and it is. But it's also a story about paths. Besides its main character, the story also mentions his brother, who isn't happy about what transpires. He's worked hard his whole life, followed the righteous path, and stuck by his good old dad. So he feels just a little gypped.

Some of us are like that good son. We don't venture away. We don't question anything. We attend church on Sundays and give our tithe. When the opportunities present, we even go on mission trips. But others take a bit more time and require greater patience. We can only love them, pray for them, and wait for them to come home.

---

11. If you need a recap but are too lazy to look up the story on your own, then here you go: A man has two sons. One goes to his dad and asks for his inheritance, and he goes off to another country and blows it all on an extravagant lifestyle. When the money dries up, he eventually goes back to his dad. And the dad responds not only with open arms but also by hosting a celebration.

Christianity is messy. Christians are messy. But Christ? He's white as snow.

Getting Social

Twitter: Tweet about something you witnessed that was done in God's name but wasn't very godly: #OhFaith.

Pinterest: Create a board called "Faith" full of amazing things people have done by faith.

Instagram: Take a picture of something that represents someone acting in faith: #F8ful.

LinkedIn: Add "Live by Faith" as a job skill and see if anyone endorses you.

Facebook: Post what faith means to you.

WhichBibleHero AreYou?

Which is your favorite guilty pleasure website?

A. poetry.org (+1)

B. sephora.com (+3)

C. ancestry.com (+5)

D. wsj.com (+7)

E. I don't have Internet access but if I did, it would be a website devoted to purchasing and selling 8-track tapes. (+9)

F. craigslist.org (+11)

Chapter Thirteen

Wise Blood

#MysteriousTrinity

1

Y ou see, you have this glass of water and you pour Coke in it, but it's still water, and . . . no that's not right. Bad example.

Let's try again. How about this: We draw a triangle. It's got three points, see, but it's still just one triangle. Okay, that doesn't work either.

How about this: One times three equals three, but one times one times one equals just one. Think of the Trinity as one times one times one, and . . . you know what? I am no good at math and have no idea what that analogy even means.

It's like . . . oh, forget it. Just accept Jesus Christ as your Savior, yeah?

So that's essentially the official Christian position on the Holy Spirit.

---

1. Postmodern symbol for Holy Trinity—or the symbol for gay rights alliance?

If you're honest, you'll probably admit that you're aware of the Holy Spirit but have absolutely no idea what, or who, he is. So you just throw the words *Holy Spirit* out there in prayer, but you aren't sure why.

The Holy Spirit makes you feel warm and fuzzy, so any time you feel all warm and fuzzy, that's the Holy Spirit. When you are on a roller coaster and you go down really fast and your stomach feels funny? Must be the Holy Spirit. The anxiety you feel as you wait for your name to be called so you can go stand in front of hundreds of people and speak? You guessed it: Holy Spirit. For good measure, let's throw in anytime you get chills down your spine; that'll be the Holy Spirit too.

The Holy Spirit is indeed mysterious and difficult to grasp. But that doesn't mean we should be satisfied with a vague description. The Holy Spirit is referenced more than 350 times in the Bible: over eighty times in the Old Testament and more than 260 in the New Testament. That means the Spirit is important—like, *really* important. So while what or who the Spirit is will remain mysterious, we can and should still get to know the Spirit.

What you know at this point is probably pretty close to the Sunday school version: Father, Son, and Holy Ghost. Beyond that, there's a ridiculously long history of Christians arguing about the Spirit; schisms have occurred over it, and cults like the Jehovah's Witnesses[2] have split with regular Christianity largely because of it.

Usually when I hear a sermon on the Holy Spirit,[3] it rambles off course rather quickly—so much so that while the sermon may have been intended as a discussion on the subject, it's really about something else, because the Holy Spirit is just too difficult to explain.

---

2. They also believe that Jesus secretly (and conveniently enough, invisibly) returned to earth in 1914, and that the "first" resurrection of people occurred in 1918—so they have a lot of issues.
3. Which in itself is rare.

There are a lot of analogies to describe him, but they just don't do him justice.

There's a crazy notion that the Christian religion was created overnight when Christ was resurrected. It wasn't. Hundreds of years of debates and divisions led to the foundations of belief. It makes sense to ask why, if Christianity is true, there are so many fights about what the Bible actually says or doesn't say.

God has never been one to just lay it all out; that's not his nature. God reveals himself to us, and in this way we are able to have a more intimate relationship with him. That's not to say God hasn't made some things plain. He has. God lays out the foundations and lets us develop the frame.

The trouble with what I've just said, however, is that it sounds like shaky theology. If you were to start building on it, you'd wind up with an unstable house. And Christianity has a lot of such houses. But it's not because God gave us a bad foundation. It's because of free will. People accept Christ, and God says, "Now here are the tools to build a relationship with me," but instead of taking those tools, people say, "It's cool, God—I've got my own tools."

Division in the church isn't anything new. Paul writes in 1 Timothy 4:1, "The Spirit clearly says that in later times some will abandon the faith and follow deceiving spirits and things taught by demons." In fact, much of the New Testament is about churches and believers who are slipping—who received God but then started adding things to their faith that ultimately were adding separation between man and God. There's a two-thousand-year history of pastors who created theology that wasn't entirely biblical; it came out of their own hearts and minds, but they presented it as revelation from God.

There will always be divisions. But God uses all things to his glory. Even in division, we can grow. Without people questioning things like the Trinity and even coming up with their own doctrines, we would not have other Christians looking at such matters more deeply and helping to form and affirm the foundations of belief. It is through division in the church that we have a stronger foundation for what it really means to be a Christian and what it means to know God.

So if God reveals himself to us, how do we know it's God and not just our mind playing tricks on us? Well, God won't reveal something apart from biblical truth. If someone says God has revealed something that only that person can properly interpret in the Scriptures, or that God has revealed to them something outside of Scripture—a hidden book, perhaps—then that's not of God. Knowing God involves reading the wealth of information he has given in the Bible and understanding it in a way that lets you be closer to him.

It's so important to read your Bible not because God wants you to know his law but because God wants you to know *him*. Yes, he reveals himself in other ways too—in the love and actions of others, for instance—but not reading the Bible means you are only understanding one part of God.

What does the Bible tell us about God? You really should read for yourself, but here's a quick starter.[4] Let's look at what the Bible reveals about God's triune nature. In Judaism, there is no Trinity. That's not to say attributes of the Trinity don't appear in the Old Testament. God reveals himself in different ways, and some Scripture passages imply Trinitarian theology. The Spirit was in the beginning (Gen. 1:2). Joshua, who led Israel after Moses, was filled with the Spirit (Deut. 34:9). The Spirit gave Samson[5] strength (Judg. 14:6). In Isaiah 61:1, the Spirit was "upon" the prophet.

In Exodus 3:14, when Moses asks God what name he should call him by, God says, "I am who I am. This is what you are to say to the Israelites: 'I am has sent me to you.'" Not very Trinitarian on the surface, but why didn't God just say "I am" once? Why three times?

In Numbers 6:24–26, God instructs Aaron and his sons to bless

---

4. And not in any way a comprehensive one. Books could be written on the attributes of God that are found in the Bible. Books have been written, actually—lots of them.
5. The Bible equivalent of He-Man.

the people with these words: "The Lord bless you and keep you; the Lord make his face shine on you and be gracious to you; the Lord turn his face toward you and give you peace." Again, why use the word *Lord* three times?

The seraphim in Isaiah 6:3 don't just say God is holy; they say, "Holy, holy, holy is the Lord Almighty; the whole earth is full of his glory." Seeing a pattern of threes?

Isaiah 48:16 says, "Come closer, and listen to this. From the beginning I have told you plainly what would happen. And now the Sovereign Lord and his Spirit have sent me with this message" (NLT). Here again is the three—first with the reference to God in the beginning, and then again to the Sovereign Lord and his Spirit.

Before considering the Spirit more, let's have a refresher on the Trinity. Here's the truth: You won't understand the triune God by a geometrical shape. You won't understand him by a diagram of a glass of water. You won't understand God through some math equation. God is not an analogy; God is God.

The church father Tertullian[6] was the first person to use the word *Trinity* to describe an attribute of God that is, frankly, beyond our understanding. Our question shouldn't be, what is the Trinity? It should be, what are the attributes of the Trinity? What does God reveal about himself?

In a very simplified nutshell, these are attributes of each person of the Trinity:

USELESS POLL

When I think about the Holy Spirit, I . . .

  A. get really confused.
  B. don't know why people act like it's so complicated.
  C. start speaking in tongues.
  D. feel more connected to God.

To be part of this poll, visit:
www.OrganicJesus.com/useless-polls

---

  6. One of the most influential theologians of the early church, Tertullian lived from 160–225.

- God the Father: The Father is most often seen in the Bible as generating things. Where the Spirit is often referenced as dwelling on earth, the Father is often seen in heaven.
- God the Son: The Son is often seen as a mediator between God and us; his action (the cross) is what brings us to God.
- God the Holy Spirit: The role of the Spirit is in some ways the most important to our earthly lives. The Spirit is often shown in the Bible as a teacher who helps us understand God, but he is also who convicts us to admit sin and help others. The role of the Spirit is often described as that of a Comforter.

Knowing the attributes of God can give us a tiny glimpse into God. It can help us grow and be closer to God. Ultimately, we simply cannot fully comprehend God, but when we know him we can experience him.

God is mysterious, but that is okay.

Perhaps you've heard one of the more popular arguments against the Trinity (albeit a weak one): that Jesus Christ never actually said he was God. A lot of people[7] make that claim, and in a way, they're right: he didn't just come out and say, "I'm God." But he did most definitely claim he was divine. Think of it like this: You're at a party, and you talk with someone about a subject you know about. "I wrote a book on that," you tell the person. Now let's say that afterward she mentions meeting you to a friend. "He's a writer," she tells him. Would the friend say, "He's not a writer unless he says, 'I am a writer.' He has to say it that way." Would you say the friend is missing the obvious?

Why didn't Jesus say he was God? He did! Over and over again—by his actions, by his authority, and by actually saying he had the same attributes as God. Jesus knew exactly who he was, and so did his followers.

Think about what Jesus did. He healed and performed miracles, yes. But even more than that, he told people, "Your sins are forgiven." That is something a man cannot do. Only God can forgive sins.

---

7. And by "people," I really mean those who like to get into religious debates.

Jesus also allowed for people to worship him. He was a good Jew; he knew what the Ten Commandments said: there is only one God, and you should worship him alone. Jesus even said this was the greatest commandment. Yet all over the Gospels, people worship Jesus. In Matthew 14:33, his disciples worship him, saying, "Truly you are the Son of God." In chapter 28, verse 9, people are worshiping him again. Read the Gospels and think about how people responded to Jesus. Did they simply treat him as a great teacher? Or did they treat him as something more— someone divine?

Here's the most important thing about the Trinity: we are called to worship God, not to understand him. So it's okay if you don't know everything about God.

WikiBreak   SHARE

What did the early believers say about the Trinity? Here are a few views:

Adoptionism: Jesus was basically man but became divine during his baptism.

Arianism: The Father is the only one who is eternal. The Son may have been with God during creation, but only because the Father created him.

Modalism: God plays different roles and has different forms but is not three distinct persons. In the early church, this view was one of the most contested. One of its many problems is that Christ prayed to the Father. But if Christ was not truly distinct from the Father, then he was essentially praying to himself.

Psilanthropism: The Son is greater than most men, but he is not God.

Today, offshoots of Christianity hold many different views on the Trinity, most of which stem from one of the above views. However, they make up a very small minority of what the rest of Christianity believes. Jehovah's Witnesses and Mormons make up the largest of the non-Trinitarian views. They believe the following:

Jehovah's Witnesses: Only the Father is God; the Son is a creation of the Father.

Mormonism: There are three distinct beings, but they are not united; they are one in purpose but not one in nature.

Common Misconceptions About the Trinity

- It consists of one person with three roles.
- Three gods transform into a super-God.
- God turned into the Son, who turned into the Spirit.
- The Trinity is not biblical.

So who is the Holy Spirit? The Spirit is indeed one of the most mysterious figures of the Bible, but that doesn't mean we can't know anything about him. First, and most important, we must know that the Spirit is equal to God; Jesus purposely says in Matthew 28:19 that we should baptize in the name of the Father and the Son and the Holy Spirit.

Great! But that doesn't really tell us a lot about him and the relationship we can have with him. So let's look at some of his attributes shown in the Bible. The Holy Spirit

- grieves (Eph. 4:30)
- loves (Rom. 15:30)
- speaks (1 Tim. 4:1)
- knows (1 Cor. 2:11)
- teaches (Luke 12:12)
- intercedes (Rom. 8:26)
- leads (Matt. 4:1)

When Jesus left the earth, the Holy Spirit came down on believers at Pentecost.[8]

But when it comes down to it, there's a lot we don't understand about the Holy Spirit. That's okay—there's also a lot we don't know about God the Father and God the Son. We only know what he

---

8. See Acts 2:1–31.

has revealed. But that by no means leaves us in the dark, because the fact is, God has told us a lot about himself. Granted, the roles of Father, Son, and Spirit can seem a little complicated, but that doesn't mean we should just forget about it. God wants us to know who he is, and that entails gaining some insight into each person of the Trinity. We shouldn't say "Father" in prayer, or cry out to Jesus, or say that we feel the Holy Spirit, without knowing why. When we understand what God has revealed to us about himself, we will be so much closer to him.

When you cry out to God, whose name do you use? Abba, Father? God? I am? Jesus? Christ? God has many names he will answer to. He's not going to say, "I didn't answer your prayer because you had the wrong name on speed dial." But using the right name in the right circumstance helps you start to understand the different roles God wants to play in your life.

We tend to approach God like we're a run-on sentence, pouring everything out. Nothing wrong with that—God loves a rambler. But when we slow down enough to think about what we are asking and how we are asking it, we begin to experience far more intimacy in our relationship with him.

Life's blessings are not dictated by getting our approach to God "right." There's no one set code of conduct that will produce a more blessed life. But I do believe the way we approach God can make us more open to receiving his wisdom, and sometimes blessings result—not because God is more willing but because we are more receptive. Though let's be clear: God doesn't promise a comfortable life full of riches. Our idea of a blessed life and God's idea may be two entirely different things.

I think the Trinity is the dumbed-down version of God—God explained in the absolute simplest form. God in his entirety—the One we will know in the next life—is far more vast and complex. But our minds are just not equipped to understand so splendid a being. Our spirits are limitless, but our minds are not. As long as our spirit remains trapped in our body, our knowledge of God will be subject to the mind's limitations.

Getting Social

Twitter: Tweet what the Holy Spirit means to you: #MysteriousTrinity.

Pinterest: Create a board called "God" full of any clippings that help you see the attributes of God.

Instagram: Take a picture of something that helps you see God's presence: #MysteriousTrinity.

LinkedIn: Add any godly attributes you have to your work-related experience.

Facebook: Post what the Holy Spirit means to you; don't reply to comments.

Which Bible Hero Are You?

If you were in college now, what would be your major?

- A. English (+1)
- B. Political science (+3)
- C. Family psychology (+5)
- D. Business (+7)
- E. Engineering (+9)
- F. College really isn't my thing. (+11)

Living on a Prayer

#PrayerfullyConfused

Praying Man   **Praying Cat**   **Praying Mantis**

Alisa[1] was one of those people who, had she been normal, would have given up on God long ago—and nobody would have blamed her. She'd had cancer several times and was seemingly always at the doctor for something rare.

Alisa was also one of the most courageous Christians I had ever known; she had no problem at all walking up to a screaming drug thug to tell him about Jesus—and no problem continuing on telling him as he threatened to kill her.

Alisa's devotion to God left her unfocused in other areas, notably driving. She wasn't a mere terrible driver. I reserve that word for drivers who just drive badly; Alisa drove psychotically.[2] For whatever reason, nobody ever bothered telling me about her driving, and

---

1. Not her real name.
2. For an appropriate animated version of how Alisa drove, refer to the

one otherwise innocent day, I found myself in the passenger seat of her car going down a residential street at freeway speeds. We dodged cars, bikes, and children as Alisa loudly sang praise songs off key. Noticing that I looked a little pale, she tried to reassure me: "I haven't been in a *bad* accident in three months."

As we neared the main city street, Alisa acknowledged, irritated, "Traffic." She looked at me and said, "We'd better start praying."

"For what?"

Alisa answered by flooring the gas pedal. With her eyes shut she prayed, "Oh Jesus, give us an opening." We needed to go left, an easy task if you stopped and were patient. But Alisa, I now understood, had absolutely no intention of stopping or even slowing down.

"Just stop! And wait!" I pleaded.

"Give us travel mercy, Jesus!"

I gripped the seat and braced for impact, wondering just how badly I'd be hurt and whether the airbags had been replaced after her last accident. There were horns and squealing tires as Alisa darted across the street like she was playing a game of Frogger.[3] Miraculously—truly miraculously—we made it.

"Praise Jesus!" Alisa said. She turned to me and asked, "Don't we have a remarkable God?"

Jesus said that if you have enough faith, you can move mountains. Alisa took this literally—too literally.

As I began thinking about prayer, it was Alisa's psychotic car behavior that first came to my mind.

Disney short "Motor Mania," featuring a peaceful everyman version of Goofy who turns into a raging lunatic as soon as he gets behind the wheel.

3. Note to young readers: Frogger was introduced in 1981 as an arcade game. Like most video games during this period, it was heavy on strategy but light on graphics (sort of the opposite of games today). The purpose was to help frogs cross a busy street full of several different hazards. If you are intimidated by the poor graphics but still want to understand the game, watch the Seinfeld episode "The Frogger" (episode 174).

Prayer comes in many forms. "Lord, don't let me die in a car crash because I'm not comfortable using the brakes" is one form. Group prayer is another.

My first experience with what I'll call a group prayer was in college. Like most college students, I felt a bit out of place and needed somewhere to belong. Campus Crusade for Christ seemed a natural choice. I was Christian and so were they.

The church youth group I had grown up with had a tendency of sticking the word *Christian* in front of whatever they were doing, which would thereby make it Christian. "Beach party" would become, for instance, "Christian beach party." The fact that nothing Christian happened at said Christian beach parties (in fact, teens tended to come home drunk from them) didn't matter.

Group prayer was a completely foreign concept to the church group of my youth, so when I was introduced to it in college, I didn't quite know what I was getting into. After an afternoon group meeting and spiritual discussion, we gathered our chairs in a circle, and before the leader of the group even finished saying, "Does anyone have any prayer requests?" nearly every hand was in the air.

My mom had been in charge of the church prayer chain years before, and I used to write down prayer request for her when she wasn't home and the call came in. I was used to prayer requests. But I wasn't used to the prayer requests that followed.

The first was for a nonbelieving friend who was having difficulty keeping up her grades because she didn't have enough time to study. Oddly, the prayer wasn't for time management—it was that she would get a good grade despite her lack of effort.

Another person worried that a younger brother might be doubting his belief because he had gotten involved with skateboarding; the actual request was for a job for the requester. (There was a one-prayer-request rule in the group, so this was a technique used by some to get in two requests.)

There were a few more requests for jobs; lots for students to do well on tests; one for a "friend" who was having impure thoughts while using the Internet. A few seemed more like opportunities to brag—like the girl who wanted to pray for the salvation of Angelina Jolie because her uncle, who worked in Hollywood, had taken her to a movie screening, where the girl had nearly bumped into Jolie's elbow and thereby established a spiritual connection.

When all the requests had been made, the leader turned to me. "And you? What would you like prayer for?"

"I'm good," I answered, intimidated. It was the first time anyone had ever asked me if I wanted them to pray for me.

This got a few chuckles. I'm not sure why. "Well, maybe next time."

Next came the prayer. The rules were simple. The person in the circle next to the leader would pray for one of the requests, and then the next person, and the next, and so on all the way back to the leader, who would close in prayer. There were about fifteen students; I would be maybe the seventh to pray.

Immediately I began to sweat. I didn't like speaking in groups, let alone praying. "Thank you for this food, God," was one of the longest prayers I had ever said in public—and that was around a dinner table with family.

The first person who prayed took about thirty seconds; each person after that seemed to be one-upping the one before by doubling his or her time of prayer. With each person it got more emotional. People in the group said, "Praise Jesus," "Thank you, Lord," and "Yes, Jesus." By the fourth person, it wasn't enough to win the Longest Prayer trophy; suddenly the language switched to Old English in a prayer fit for the King James Bible.

Everyone in the room seemed to be experiencing the Spirit. Soon there were even moans, and it began to seem a little . . . orgasmic. The "Mmm, yes, Lord" got more and more sensual.

As the circle of prayers worked its way toward me, I started to ignore what was being said and tried to rehearse in my head what I would say. I wanted to sound real, but I didn't know how.

When my turn finally came, I took a deep breath and said, "Dear God, thank you for letting us come together to bring these requests, and I just ask that you hear them and take care of us and amen." I was out of breath when I finished, and all I could think about was where the nearest water fountain was.

In Matthew 6:5, Jesus says we shouldn't be boastful in prayer—that we should pray in private. It seems like the perfect excuse to write of the experience I've described as not biblically grounded. But the more I thought about prayer, the more I was reminded that this kind of prayer brings about something the Bible mentions a lot: fellowship. Our private prayers help us in our personal growth. But personal growth is only one piece of the Christian pie. Fellowship helps us become accountable and even more spiritual.

I was beginning to realize that there was something worse than not being able to pray in a group: not being able to pray at all.

What are your eyes doing during prayer?

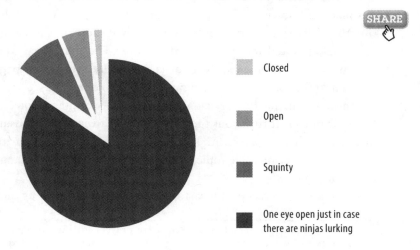

Closed

Open

Squinty

One eye open just in case there are ninjas lurking

Note: This information is based on complex, inconclusive evidence based on research done in my head.

Prayer is simple—in theory.

To most people, prayer works kind of like this: You tell God what you want. Then you act like a good boy or girl and you wait for it to happen. Then finally you complain when it doesn't.

In theory this isn't completely wrong. But it's also not completely right.

Christians are taught a lot of things—how to give, how to live, what to teach children.

Prayer is often seen as a natural instinct: you don't need to teach someone how to pray. But that's not true. Our relationship with God starts when we learn how to communicate with him. But we do need to learn. Instincts eventually kick in once we understand prayer, but we still have to lay the foundation.

As I considered my own prayer life, I thought about Alisa. I had never prayed like that. My prayers have always been a bit bland and uneventful.

To learn more about how to pray, I turned to the most obvious place of knowledge: Google. For added effect, I considered hitting the "I feel lucky" button but ultimately decided not to chance it. Google pointed me in several directions. The first three were, of course, advertisements; as it turns out, there are *lots* of pages devoted to the topic of prayer, some Christian, some not.

One page in particular caught my eye: a website devoted to Catholic prayer. It turns out there are actually over three thousand different Catholic prayers. As I looked through the list, which covered nearly every possible topic,[4] I thought about what Jesus taught us about prayer.

He did want to teach us how to pray, but he didn't give us thou-

---

4. I'm not kidding—every topic. There were prayers for the unemployed, prayers for renewal, prayers for after confession, and even a "Universal Prayer for All Things Necessary to Salvation," which should leave you covered in case of basically anything.

sands of different prayers to get us started. He gave us only one: The
Lord's Prayer.

Obviously that prayer is important. Here it is:

Our Father in heaven,
hallowed be your name.
your kingdom come,
your will be done,
    on earth, as it is in heaven.
Give us today our daily bread.
And forgive us our debts,
    as we also have forgiven our debtors.
And lead us not into temptation,
    but deliver us from the evil one. [5]

I have said that prayer literally thousands of times. But I have not
stopped to think about it once. If Jesus gave only one prayer, then
maybe—just maybe—I should stop saying it and start dwelling on it.

It starts off innocently enough: God is in heaven and is in control
of all things in this universe. There's something important about
that opening; it's not just about God being in control. In the Old
Testament, God went by many names—El Elohim, El Shaddai,
Adonai, Elyon, and others—but Jesus tells us to use the personal
expression "Father." He wants our prayer to be intimate, relational.

Jesus says that God's will is to be done not only in heaven but
also on earth, meaning that God is not just someone we meet after
we die—he is with us right now, here in our daily life. We're to ask
him for our daily necessities, Jesus tells us, including forgiveness for
our sins, contingent on our showing others mercy. [6] It's Jesus's polite
way of telling us, don't be asking God for favors while you're

---

5. The prayer appears here in its long form, taken from Matthew 6:9–13.
    You can find it in its short form in Luke 11:2–4.
6. Awkward silence here as I pause to consider what I have done for others.

treating others like dirt. Finally, we're to ask God to take control of our life and keep us free from harm.

The Lord's Prayer is in many ways a CliffsNotes version of Jesus's entire ministry. It puts us in a childlike state and makes us look at God as a child would a father; it calls us to do good and to forgive; and it acknowledges that God is in control of all things.

While the Lord's Prayer is the only time Jesus actually gave us an example of how to pray, Luke 5:16 tells us that Jesus prayed often. He prayed for two very important reasons: to communicate with God and to be an example.

If we become a believer but don't learn how to pray, then our prayers are more like shouts. We are shouting distantly at God in heaven, doing everything to be heard. And he does hear us, even our whispers. But we don't hear back. He answers us, but when we don't understand prayer, we create a disconnection between him and us.

A few years ago, Diana and I spent our wedding anniversary in Rome. We got spiritual one day and took what was being called the "Christian" tour of Rome. It took us to several churches and the catacombs.[7]

The tour ended at the Scala Sancta, which supposedly are the steps Jesus climbed on the way to his trial. The popes loved to bring stuff from Jerusalem to Rome, and the steps were brought there, as the story goes, one by one in AD 326.[8] I didn't go up the stairs;

---

7. In ancient days, the Romans would incinerate the dead. This didn't sit well with Christians who wanted to bury their dead. Unfortunately, due to health concerns, they couldn't bury corpses in the city, so they took them outside the city and buried them in the catacombs, which are essentially underground caverns for the dead.

8. As a side note, the church with stairs that lead to nowhere is odd, but it's by far not the strangest (and creepiest) thing in Rome. That distinction is reserved for the Capuchin Crypt. From the outside, it looks innocent enough. It's just a little church named Santa Maria della Concezione die

instead, I watched as people got on their knees and said a ritual prayer with each step until they reached the top. I'm sure the experience meant a lot to them, but I couldn't help but wonder what the prayer proved.

How we pray shouldn't be mocked.[9] We connect with God in different ways. But we shouldn't be told how to pray. One of the first prayers recorded in the Old Testament is when Abraham cried to God. Prayer is nothing more than that connection.

In the Bible, the disciples asked Jesus to teach them how to pray. He responded when they humbled themselves by asking how to do something that some might have said should have been natural.

When I was a freshman in high school, my grandma called me and asked if I'd stay at her house with my great grandma while she and my grandpa went out of town. My great grandmother, or Granny as we called her, was ninety years old but perfectly fine on

---

Cappuccini. The dirty little secret under the church is what will send shivers down your spine. In 1631, monks came to the church with three hundred cartloads of deceased friars. Instead of doing the normal thing of burying them, they decided, why not make an artistic shrine of sorts for them. So they began nailing them to the walls in pretty patterns, turning them into light fixtures (yes, the bones of deceased friars were turned into lights) and doing other things that you should not do with bones. In total, over four thousand bodies are on display for all the paying public to see. It's horrifying, it's bizarre, and it smells. Never before and never since have I seen anything so morbidly disturbing.

9. As we left the church, Diana discovered that her camera had been stolen below those beloved stairs. Perhaps we should have prayed just a little harder and maybe taken the climb ourselves instead of quietly mocking those who did?

---

her own; my grandma just felt more comfortable knowing someone was there with her.

I agreed because my mom promised me I could go to the video store and rent a video game to play at the house. I chose one of the bloodiest and most violent games around: *Mortal Kombat*. By today's standards, the game would be considered a family selection, but at the time it was rare for something to be so brutal.

As I played the game, Granny stood behind me and watched, but didn't say anything. When I finished the fight, she asked if she could play.

Despite having a bit of arthritis in her hands, she was able to fight well and caught on to the fighting game quickly. After the game she said, "It's a little violent."

I nodded. "That's why it's good."

"I used to live next to violent neighbors in Texas. They were named Bonnie and Clyde."

I turned quickly interested. "The robbers?"

She nodded and let out a drawn-out "Yep."[10]

She had other things she could be doing, but she chose to continue to play the video game with me. It was her way of submitting herself to a childlike state to bond with me.

She let me control the rest of the afternoon; we ate what I wanted and watched the movies that I wanted.

In the evening, I went to the guest bedroom and began reading, and Granny went to her room as well. About thirty minutes into the book, I heard a voice. I crept quietly down the hall and peeked into her room. Granny was sitting in her old rocker with her eyes closed, praying.

Unnoticed, I stayed in the hall and listened. She prayed for each person in my family. But it wasn't like normal prayer. It was like she was speaking to God. It was a humble prayer. And it was the first time I understood that you could talk to God.

At the time I didn't take much away from it. I was in high school

---

10. My mom told me later she was probably just confused.

but still a child. But I never forgot that night. Nearly twenty years later, it was one of the first things I thought of when I considered how to pray. Granny did two things. She prayed alone. And she prayed to God the same way a person would talk to her friend on the phone.[11]

We often make prayer a one-sided conversation with God in which we do all the talking. We take a deep breath, say as much as is humanly possible in that one breath, and then say amen. It's not a meditation; we don't listen for God's answer. But Granny paused and listened. She didn't just talk to God. She let God talk back.

Granny's was the kind of prayer Jesus was teaching when he taught us to pray—the kind in which you are slow to speak and quick to listen. You let the Spirit move the prayer along rather than just pray for what you want.

WikiBreak

When I was in high school, a church near us opened and had prayer vigils for its first week. Day and night, dozens would show up to pray over the church. It was the first time I had ever heard of such devotion.

Devoted as those folks were, they come nowhere close to holding the continuous prayer vigil record. That title belongs to the Moravian Church (which is actually a denomination, not a church), which prayed uninterrupted twenty-four hours a day—for one hundred years. The Moravian Church owes everything to a little-known monk named Alexander, founder of the Acoemetae order of monks. They are the original kings of prayer. They held vigils day and night for the lifespan of the movement.

America, not to be outdone, is doing its best to one-up them all. In Kansas City, Missouri, a mission organization has created the IHOP of ministry: The International House of Prayer. Since 1999, the organization has had worship teams praying 24/7.

---

11. Or if you're a younger reader, text a friend. But seriously, pick up the phone every now and then and actually talk to people to remind yourself that they are human.

There's a problem with prayer that you don't experience when life is good. You experience it when life is not good: your prayers go unanswered.

The Bible says in Matthew 21:21–22, "Truly I tell you, if you have faith and do not doubt, not only can you do what was done to the fig tree, but also you can say to this mountain, 'Go, throw yourself into the sea,' and it will be done. If you believe, you will receive whatever you ask for in prayer."

That's great! So why did your best friend die of cancer? Why did you not win the lottery? Why did you not get that promotion?

It's obvious, of course: your prayer was not answered because you lacked faith! If only you would have believed just a little bit harder, then that five-year-old would have pulled through. So shame on you.

Unless there's more to faith and answered prayer than that. How do you get the kind of faith Jesus described? Because you can't fake it. There is no formula. If God doesn't provide it, does that mean that you just don't get it? That another kind of faith is required?

One thing is certain: God's not about adding to your hardship by saying, "It's all your fault for not believing hard enough!" It's not up to you to "get it right"—it's just up to you to get with God, the way Jesus got with his Father in prayer. Prayer isn't about trying to get a shortcut to the problem you are facing—it's about getting connected to God. When you do, God may in fact give you the kind of faith that gets a miracle in response. He does do that; specific answers to specific prayers are real. But you can't make it happen. And the grace that sees you through life's losses and struggles is also real. The apostles experienced both realities, and so have Jesus's followers through the ages, and so will you.

Alisa may have been a prayer warrior, but sometimes she was praying for her will to be done and not God's will. We all are guilty of this. That's why it's so important for our prayers to become conversational. When we not only talk to God but *listen* to him—when we hear his voice—that's when we can move mountains.

Jesus provided the best example of how we should pray, the Bible gives us plenty of others. In 1 Samuel 1, Hannah prays for a son, proving it's okay to ask for things we want. Daniel prays a confession in Daniel 9:1–19; Habakkuk prays a joyful song in Habakkuk 3; Jehoshaphat prays for deliverance (2 Chron. 20:5–12); and Nehemiah prays for success (Neh. 1:5–11).

There is no one true and perfect prayer, but all prayer starts as communication with God.

I was too young and immature to realize that Granny had given me one of my best life lessons—that prayer is talking with God. Later in life, when I began finding quiet places and making that discovery, my spiritual life got better.

Faith is a journey. It's full of doubts. Questions. Confusion. And God can take all of that and use it for your good and his glory—if you don't close yourself off to him.

It starts with prayer. That's where God—the historical one whom we only know through the Bible—starts to get real. In my youth, prayer was a quick little jingle before bed. That's certainly one of prayer's many forms, but when I slowed the jingle down and prayed as if I were actually conversing with God, things got a little more holy. God's voice didn't boom down from the heavens; it didn't have to. When you let God speak, you hear him in your heart—even when it's something you don't want to hear.

But conversational prayer doesn't start and end in a quiet place. It can take place anywhere. In all situations, pray. If people stopped more often to say a quick prayer (even with their eyes open, so others didn't know) before speaking, then more of life's problems could be solved. If you pause when your frustration is at its peak and spend just thirty seconds or so to let God calm you down, your day will go better.

When we begin to see prayer as a conversation between ourselves and God, then it becomes easier to talk to God throughout the day, just as we would talk to a friend.

Getting Social

Twitter: Tweet a prayer with the hashtag #PrayerfullyConfused. Remember to keep your prayer under 140 characters.

Pinterest: Start a collection of photos of animals that appear to be praying.

Instagram: Take a picture of something or someone you are praying for.

LinkedIn: Add "prayer warrior" as a job skill.

Facebook: On every friend's post for the last twenty-four hours, leave the comment, "I'm praying for you."

WhichBibleHero **Are**You?

What is your car of choice?

A. Something cute (+1)

B. A hybrid (+3)

C. The brand I've driven since I was a teen (+5)

D. Something with bling (+7)

E. A clown car (+9)

F. Something that goes off-road (+11)

Epilogue

Organic Faith

#AtPeaceWithGod

@God:
Now What?

SHARE

Death comes to all of us. We can build up whatever masks we want to shield ourselves from it, and try not to be afraid of it, but it's going to come. And when it does, if all we have to show for it is our personal satisfaction, then we will indeed be dead.

But what if we lived for something greater than ourselves? What if we left a legacy? What if we did as the Bible commands and *loved*, putting the well-being of others over our own?

The Internet left me feeling distant from God, but it is also what ultimately led me to seek God out again—to begin my quest for the Organic Jesus. God isn't asking us to cut the cord to the Internet. God is asking us to take a journey. He invites us to let the Holy Spirit come alive in us and use us as his vessels.

Discovering Jesus means you have found a path to happiness that has absolutely nothing to do with yourself. It's about God. Many people claim to know God. But go into any church and ask yourself how many people there are really Christians. Many of them read something in a book called the Bible and happen to believe in it, but how many actually practice it? Reading a book is easy; doing what it says is hard. Anyone can read a book about baseball, but that doesn't make them a baseball player. It doesn't make them anything.

The Bible is a complicated book. It is often misinterpreted, abused, and used in ways never intended for it. But there's no way to misinterpret Jesus's ultimate message: love. Love God. Love others. That is the whole duty of man. When you consider just those two things—loving God and loving others—the Bible begins to read a whole lot differently. And that's the thing about the Bible: It evolves in our understanding. It reshapes. It becomes something entirely different. It's indeed a wondrous thing, because no other book can do that.

But while people refer to the Bible as the Word of God—and it is—God is beyond the Bible. He cannot be contained in one book or a million books. So if your relationship with God is based only on reading the Bible, then look further, because that in itself won't transform you. It didn't transform Joseph Stalin, who is said to have memorized the entire New Testament. Reading the Bible didn't make him a Christian, and it won't make you one (not that you're anything like Stalin!). You've got to actually practice what it preaches. And what it proclaims is faith in Jesus that expresses itself in love for God and love for others.

Don't take my word that God is real. There's no scientific proof of God. You can't just say, "Hey God—'sup?" To believe in God seems a little out of this world. So you shouldn't believe anyone who says God is real—or anyone who says he isn't—just because that person says so. Not your pastor, your friend, your parent, your child, your spouse, or anyone else. You should challenge God himself to challenge you. You should search for him on your own. Take your own journey. So many people fall in faith because they rely on other people who ultimately disappoint them. That kind of faith cannot endure—not when it rests on fallible humans. Faith endures when you ground it in the certainty of truth that you yourself discover, not truth that others discover for you.

We have lived the past several decades in what might be aptly called a sound-bite Christianity. What people today know about Christianity and Christians does not come by way of the gospels or even books about Christianity; it comes from sound bites on YouTube or TV in which this Christian and that one says something remarkably dumb. We have to start living beyond the sound bites. We need to live lives so full of the glory of Christ that his resplendence shocks people into actually investigating beyond the sound bites.

WikiBreak   SHARE

You've probably heard about missionaries around the world who have devoted their lives to spreading the message of the gospel. But what is the history behind missions?

It really all goes back to a divine man who walked the face of the earth two thousand years ago. His name was Jesus of Nazareth, and he gave his followers a lot of great messages. One was called the Great Commission (Matt. 28:16–20). He didn't say that those who were called to do so should become missionaries—he said that every single follower of his name should do so.

"Gulp! So you mean I actually have to serve people through the mission field if I want to be a Christian?" No—and yes. No, your salvation doesn't hinge on you getting baptized and then heading for the Congo (though God might send you there—who knows?). But yes, every follower of Jesus is meant to be involved in mission work. So let's clarify what that means, because missions come in many forms. There are mission opportunities all around you—as far away as Nepal; as near as the block you live on. The important thing is, you have a part to play in spreading God's kingdom in this world. How and where is for you and God to determine. But one thing is certain: wherever you go, whether near or far, there are people who need to know the Jesus you know. And God is sending you to introduce those people to him.

The disciples were the first missionaries, and after them, the disciples of the disciples. Throughout the first century they went all over Europe and Northern Africa. By AD 300, the Bible had already been translated into ten languages; today it has been translated into more than six hundred. As the church grew and expanded, missionaries were usually monks who went around the world and built monasteries.

The mission field that we know today is largely the product of a Baptist-minister-turned-missionary named William Carey. In 1792 he published a manifesto of sorts called "An Enquiry into the Obligations of Christians to Use Means for the Conversion of Heathens." The title may be a little—let's just say, insensitive—but his heart was in the right place. It included a plan for action to reach areas of the world that had essentially been forgotten. He created a mission society and packed up for India, where he became one of the country's greatest missionaries.

When you are preaching to a part of the world that has never seen another race, let alone heard of Jesus, you need more than Bible verses—you need devotion. Adoniram Judson went to Burma to preach the Word. After twelve years, he had converted eighteen people. But he didn't give up. By the time of his death he had established over one hundred churches and led thousands to Christ.

God doesn't call us because we are extraordinary people; he calls us because he can make us extraordinary people. Jesus didn't change millions of lives; Jesus changed the lives of twelve people—twelve people who accepted his grace and took it to the world, started a movement of love and peace, and died for the cause. Twelve people who were far from extraordinary; who were not even ordinary; who, you might even say, were cowardly. They weren't scholars of the Bible. They probably weren't very educated at all. Yet God took those twelve and made them extraordinary. He gave them gifts that only by his grace could they ever have possessed.

He can do this for each of us. But first we have to forget everything we were taught, everything we see on TV and the Internet, everything we read—we have to cast it all aside and let God reveal himself to us personally.

"Personal Jesus": when you accept Jesus into your life, you probably hear that a lot. Even if you're not a Christian, you've probably heard it plenty. It's a nice expression. Really sums things up—until people start talking, telling you what it means to have a personal relationship with Jesus. Often, something seems to be missing from their description. Because "personal Jesus" has a word in it that a lot of people forget—*personal*. God doesn't want you to have the same relationship with him as Joe the Plumber down the street. Each of us is unique. You are unique, and he wants to have a relationship with you that reflects your uniqueness.

Life is sometimes a little . . . backwards.

But backwards is okay.

Life is crazy. It is backwards. Upside down. But that's how you experience God. Not in moments of sanity. It's when everything is pulled apart and doesn't make sense. God is there. God is waiting. Find God.

Getting Social

Twitter: Tweet what God means to you in an Internet/social-media-driven world: #AtPeaceWithGod.

Pinterest: Can clipping and sharing things bring you closer to God? Think about it. If it can, then start a board to prove it.

Instagram: Take a picture of something that reminds you of a charitable cause. Post a link to where people can find out more information.
LinkedIn: Look at your LinkedIn page. Do your job skills match your talents as a Christian? Don't quit your job or anything, but maybe there's something you can do at work that better represents your skills.
Facebook: If someone looked at your Facebook page, would they know that you are a follower of Christ, or would that shock them a little? If it would shock them, perhaps reconsider what you post on your wall next.

Which Bible Hero Are You?

If you went to a party, what would your attire accomplish?

    A. Make people ask what designer I was wearing (+1)

    B. Get me on the best-dressed list (+3)

    C. Help me blend in (+5)

    D. Make people think I'm a business leader (+7)

    E. Make people laugh at how outrageous I look (+9)

    F. Turn heads (+11)

Acknowledgments

I acknowledge the following:

There are many holes in the Kennedy assassination.

Library should be pronounced "li-barry" or "li-berry" to any librarian.

Toothpaste should be pushed out from the bottom, not the middle.

Silence is golden, but golden is not silence.

Over seven hundred million people can't read; the rest of the world population chooses not to.

McDonald's sells an estimated 6 million hamburgers a day; over twenty thousand people die per day of hunger-related causes.

Diana deserves more than I could ever give her credit for and I am thankful every day that God put us together and made me forever blessed.

It's easy to forget that things could have turned out a lot differently if I had been born to another set of parents. While I can't help but wonder what things would have been like if my father's first name was Bill and his last name was Gates, I know my parents showered me with love and the grace of God. I may not have billions, but I have a coupon for a free drink at Chipotle and know my place in the world—so thanks, Mom and Dad, for the Chipotle coupon. And thanks for making sure that when I was dropped on my head, it was never on the soft part. But most of all, thanks for raising me in an environment that made me certain of who I am and what I was called to do.

I acknowledge that I *kind of* like One Direction.[1]

Like so many books, this book was destined for the literary grave, not for lack of quality but for lack of anyone willing to take

---

1. Kind of.

a chance. I acknowledge that I am forever grateful to my agent, Dan Balow, and his persistent efforts not only to give me a chance, but also to not give up when others would have.

I acknowledge that the team at Kregel Publications merit more thanks than I can give them here.

I acknowledge the truly gifted and talented artist Guadalupe Rivas, who created most of the illustrations for this book.

The world is nothing without teachers. During my junior and senior years of college, I had the honor and privilege of studying the Bible as literature under Dr. Jane Hipolito. A brand-new dimension of the Bible was opened to me, and I acknowledge that I am forever thankful to her for the things I learned.

And, of course, I acknowledge that it is only by the grace of God that I'm not working the night shift at a twenty-four-hour donut shop. I spent my entire education in remedial classrooms, failed my high school reading test, and was told to go to trade school—and yet somehow I ended up with two bachelor's degrees, a master's, and a handful of published books. God likes underdogs, because underdogs truly know it is only by God's miraculous abilities that they can get where they are. The one thing I never should have been is the one thing that God made me.

Thank you. That is all.

Discussion Questions

Introduction: Organic Jesus

1. How have you changed since you became a Christian? If you are not a Christian, how have you changed from ten years ago?
2. Do you see "holes" in Christianity? What are they?
3. What distractions keep you from growing?
4. The author mentions a children's Bible is what eventually helped him get closer to God; what has helped you grow closer? If you aren't a Christian, what have you read, watched, or participated in as you seek answers?
5. What do you think Jesus meant when he said, "The kingdom of heaven belongs to children"?

Chapter 1: The Passion of the Jew

1. Do you think Jesus Christ is a Savior? A historic figure? Or something else?
2. There have been lots of artistic and cinematic portrayals of Jesus; what is your portrayal of him? What did he look like? How did he act? Pretend you are describing him to someone who has never heard of him.
3. What is your favorite portrayal of Jesus? It can be a film, song, painting, book, or something else entirely.
4. Is there anything you learned about Jesus as a child that you came to question as an adult? Where did your childhood understanding of Jesus come from?
5. Do you have or did you ever have doubts about God or Jesus? Did you or do you seek answers to those doubts? If you've never had doubts, then where do you think they come from for other people?

Chapter 2: Will the Real Jesus Please Step Up?

1. What gives you the faith to believe that Jesus Christ is the Messiah? If you don't think he is, what makes you doubt?

2. How do we know Jesus is the Messiah and not just a great teacher?

3. Jesus said he was God, but not in that direct way. Why don't you think Christ ever said, "I am God"?

4. Do you believe Jesus is God? Why or why not?

5. C. S. Lewis famously said in *Mere Christianity* that some people believe Jesus was a great moral teacher but reject his claim to be God—he argues that those people basically believe a great teacher is also utterly insane. There have been plenty of scientists who are brilliant but also crazy; do you believe the same is true for a philosopher-teacher such as Jesus? Could he have been a great moral teacher while also being insane?

Chapter 3: Does God Have a Pinky Toe?

1. Have you ever asked yourself if you are crazy for believing in God? What helped put doubts aside?

2. First Peter 3:15 says that we should always be prepared to give a reason for the hope that we have. Do you feel prepared to give a reason for the hope you have? If not, what would it take for you to feel prepared?

3. How do you think science and God can coexist?

4. The author says, "It would not be far off to say that Christianity contributed more to the rise of atheism than any other cause. Science did not create atheism—Christians did." How true do you think that statement is? Do you know a nonbeliever whose doubts have been shaped by the poor actions of Christians?

5. The author says, "The Christian faith isn't so much a lifestyle as a journey." What does this mean to you? How is faith a journey?

Chapter 4: 50 Shades of Bible

1. Do you think the Bible can be a myth but also true? Explain.
2. Does the Bible feel dated to you? What, if anything, helps you make sense of it for life today?
3. The author mentions literary patterns in the Bible; do you think those patterns are important? Do they change the way you read or think about the Bible?
4. Why do you think the apocryphal books are or are not important?
5. What are some of your favorite Christian books or movies?

Chapter 5: History of the World, Part 2

1. Why are there thousands of different religions in the world today?
2. How do you know you believe in the right one?
3. Have you ever been on a mission trip—long or short? How did it change or shape you? If you have never been, what is holding you back? How can you make it happen?
4. Were you spiritually prepared for adulthood? If not, how could you have been more prepared?
5. Christ calls us to believe in him—why should we even bother going to church? We can worship God anywhere and there's no "thou shall go to church" commandment.

Chapter 6: East of Eden

1. Do you believe this statement: "There is no greater advocate for satan than some Christians"? Explain.
2. The author asks this question in the book: "If Christianity is so great that the very Spirit of God indwells believers, then why are so many Christians so flawed?" Why do you think so many Christians are flawed?
3. If a Christian believes in Christ but does not do good deeds, are they saved? Explain.
4. Have you ever been disappointed by a Christian? To what

do you attribute their disappointing words or actions—is it a flaw in their religion, their faith, or their person?

5. What does it mean to you to have a relationship with God?

Chapter 7: Can You Put That Miracle in the Form of a Pill?

1. Have you ever personally witnessed or experienced something you cannot explain? If so, describe the situation. Are you content with leaving it unexplained?

2. The Bible says Jesus did all kinds of miracles, but it only tells us about thirty-seven. Why do you think there aren't written accounts of the other miracles?

3. Of the miracles written about in the Bible, which one do you most frequently think about? What is it about that miracle that makes it so memorable?

4. Why do you think God seems to answer some prayers but not others?

5. What is a "spiritual healing"?

Commercial Break: Interview with an Atheist

1. Have you ever talked to a nonbeliever about why they didn't believe? What reasons did they give?

2. Was there anything in the interview in the book that surprised or jumped out at you?

3. Roland believes that humans define moral code. Do you think this is possible? Why or why not?

4. Roland mentioned for him to believe in God it would basically take the actual presence of God descending like a hand from the sky. Why doesn't God reveal himself that way?

5. There are more atheists today than ever before. Why do you think that is?

Chapter 8: Natura-Diddily

1. What is the most difficult thing in your life that you have faced? How did you get through it?

2. Why do you think bad things happen?

3. In Matthew 21:21, Jesus says if our faith is strong then we can tell a mountain to move into the sea and it will obey. So why do bad things happen even when we pray for them not to?

4. If you know a friend is hurting, are you comfortable talking to them? Do you ever keep quiet for fear of saying the wrong thing?

5. Do you cling to the hurting as a way to make you appreciate your own life? Do you wait to see if the hurting say what they need, or do you help in some way without being asked, even at the risk of not being helpful?

Chapter 9: Would Jesus Take a Selfie?

1. What was church like for you as a child?

2. Who in your life has served as a type of mentor?

3. The author says that "there's only one way, one path to salvation, and it has absolutely nothing to do with who you are, what you've done, or what you do." Do you struggle with the idea of grace—that God gives you salvation in spite of anything you have or have not done?

4. Was there a pivotal moment in your life when you began to grow spiritually? What prompted the change?

5. Why do so many scandals begin in the church?

Chapter 10: Love in a Time of Cholera

1. What do you think Jesus meant when he said, "I did not come to bring peace, but a sword" (Matt. 10:34)?

2. For a gospel that preaches love, why do you think there are so many Christian groups that preach a gospel of hate and condemnation?

3. Do you think Christianity is supposed to be "fun"? The author says that "sometimes we put so much emphasis on enjoying life that we forget what we were called to do." How do you find balance between enjoying life and doing what

God has called you to do? How do you make what you are
called to do enjoyable?

4. What does grace mean to you?

5. The author says that spiritual growth often happens when
   we start getting a little uncomfortable and doing things we
   don't normally do. How can you get a little uncomfortable
   spiritually?

Chapter 11: Christian Hard Rock

1. What do you think when you hear the words *Christian
   worship*?

2. How do you worship God?

3. The author describes a portrait of the early church that isn't
   completely like we know today; ideally, what do you think
   church should look like?

4. Regarding church worship, the author asks, "How do we
   know what's authentic and what just feels good? That the person onstage isn't leading us to experience something based on
   fakery? How do we know the church we attend has the same
   background and foreground?" How would you answer that?

5. In what ways do you worship God when you aren't at church?

Chapter 12: What the Faith!

1. What do you think about the end times?

2. Why do you think so many people are fascinated by end-time
   prophecy?

3. Do you believe in angels and demons? What role do you think
   they play?

4. Is there Christian theology that you struggle with or are confused by?

5. The author says we are all on a path to return to God, but
   everyone's path looks different; what does your path look like
   right now? Are you questioning? Doubting? Serving? Just trying to get by?

Chapter 13: Wise Blood

1. How would you describe the Holy Spirit?
2. How would you describe the Trinity?
3. God uses all things to his glory—can you think of something bad that happened that God used to his glory?
4. How do you think division in the church has made the church stronger?
5. Do you think we can ever really know God? Why or why not?

Chapter 14: Living on a Prayer

1. Are you comfortable praying aloud, by yourself? In a small group? Before a large group?
2. How would you describe your prayer life?
3. Were you ever taught to pray? If not, how did you learn?
4. How does prayer connect us to God?
5. Is it okay to pray for things we want?

Epilogue: Organic Faith

1. What aspects of death scare you?
2. How do you practice what the Bible says?
3. Have you ever sought God out in an attempt to prove to yourself that God is real? What did that look like? What was the result?
4. How can God make you an extraordinary Christian?
5. What does having a "personal relationship with Jesus Christ" mean?

Judaism   Monotheistic religion that began in the fifteenth century. It teaches the equality of all and believes we should have oneness with God. Prayer is an important part of spiritual life and helps connect you with God.

Islam   Polytheistic religion believed to have begun in 1400 BC. Its principal beliefs are found in a set of texts known as the Vedas. You create your own destiny based on your actions.

Hinduism   Monotheistic religion that began in the seventh century. Followers seek to keep the five pillars (confession of faith, prayer, alms [giving money to needy causes], fasting, and pilgrimage). You must submit to God. There will be a resurrection of the dead, and people will go to either paradise or hell.

Buddhism   Monotheistic religion that began in the 1800s in the Middle East. Its name means "The Glory of God." Believes that God sends messengers to reveal himself to humans, and that all humanity and all religions are united under one God.

Shintoism   Monotheistic religion founded in the nineteenth century. Promotes the "Joyous Life," which can come from acts of charity. Believes that the body is only borrowed.

Sikhism   Pantheistic religion that began in 600 BC. It teaches nonviolence and believes that all people have a soul, which creates its own destiny. We should learn to control our mind, because our mind can bring us away from our soul. The ultimate goal is liberation of the soul.

Baháʼí   Monotheistic religion believed to be founded during the Bronze Age. Follows thirteen principles of faith. Believes that we need to sanctify our life to have a closer relationship with God.

Jainism   Began in the 1900s. Followers believe that its prophets were destined to save mankind from suffering. Believes in aiding the poor over building fancy shrines; religious ceremonies should be simple and modest, because money is better spent helping the poor.

Hòa Hảo   Polytheistic religion that literally means "the way of gods." Believes that spirits live in all natural places. Prior to World War II, it was the main religion of Japan.

Tenriism   One of the few religions that does not say whether there is or isn't a supreme being. Teaches that bad actions bring bad consequences and, similarly, good actions bring good consequences. The ultimate goal is to reach a state where you free yourself of suffering, which happens by getting rid of greed, hatred, and ignorance.

Which Bible Hero Are You?

Quiz Results

Add up all your points and see which hero you are. Share your results with your friends by visiting www.OrganicJesus.com/bible-hero-quiz.

15–29: I Am . . . King David

You have a gentle spirit—unless you are faced up against giants, in which case you strike them down for your king. Your harmonies can give rest to the restless. You are creative and poetic with your words. You seek God in all your trials and take pleasure in his presence. You may not look fit to lead, but the quality of leadership is within you. It's possible that you have a thing for other guys' wives, so be careful with that one—you are absolutely not allowed to kill a husband to have his wife.

Share your results by visiting: www.OrganicJesus.com/king-david.

30–59: I Am . . . Esther

If you happen to be a guy, don't fret this one—you're just ubersexual; women are gonna love you. That being said—ladies, little girls dream of being princesses, but you dream of being queen. You understand the value of beauty but find greater pleasure in being in a position to change the world. You are the type of person who knows her place in the world, and you are confident even in situations that could lead to your ultimate demise. You value the wisdom of your family and will stop at nothing to protect them. You also smell good—really good; you're not the kind who pours on cheap perfume and then feels surprised when people gag in your pungent presence. You wear the organic stuff that makes a room smell like a rose garden as soon as you walk in.

Share your results by visiting: www.OrganicJesus.com/esther.

60–84: I Am . . . Ruth

The Mother-in-Law is going to adore you. You are pretty much the most loyal person anyone will ever meet. When you have a friend, you'll never leave her side. While other people go for looks in a potential mate, you value much deeper things. You may be in a place where people wouldn't look down on you for staying home and basically doing nothing, but you choose instead to go out in the field and get a little dirty. You might have a bit of a foot fetish, but no one is going to judge you for it.

Share your results by visiting: www.OrganicJesus.com/ruth.

85–114: I Am . . . Moses

People who know you have a running gag about how horrible you are with directions. You aren't necessarily the best leader, but you have people around you with leadership qualities that help you stand out. You stand up against the injustices of the powerful inflicted on the powerless. You are willing to leave a position of wealth and fortune for God. You may or may not talk to God by way of burning plants. You hate manna.

Share your results by visiting: www.OrganicJesus.com/moses.

115–144: I Am . . . Noah

Strangers think you're crazy. Your friends think you're crazy. Heck, even you know you're crazy. The crazy thing about your being crazy? You aren't crazy. A little eccentric, perhaps, and you may be the type that likes to pull off to the side of the road to admire rainbows—especially double rainbows. But you are definitely not crazy. You aren't afraid of any wild idea when it comes from God. When people try to detour you, you keep on going without a second thought. When it comes to God, you are driven. No matter the size of the project, you have it covered. You might find yourself getting a little tipsy every now and then, so just make sure you keep your robe tied.

Share your results by visiting: www.OrganicJesus.com/noah.

145–165: I Am . . . Rahab

You have a bit of a . . . naughty side. But God uses you to show that everyone has a place in his kingdom. You welcome God's people into your home, and you aid them when they face harm. Your works are applauded, but they also surprise people because you don't give the impression that you would be so caring. You value God because you fear him, but also you know he can get you out of bad situations.

Now let's get it out in the open: if you are a prostitute, then it's time to let God find you a new profession.

Share your results by visiting: www.OrganicJesus.com/rahab.

About the Author

Scott Douglas wrote this About page, which, he admits, makes him sound a bit like a narcissist. So, narcissistically speaking, Douglas is the esteemed author of a memoir about his experiences working in a public library (*Quiet, Please: Dispatches from a Public Librarian*); an ongoing YA series (*The N00b Warriors*); and two technical books on iPhone app development (*Going Mobile* and *Build Your Own Apps for Fun and Profit*).

Douglas teaches humor and memoir writing for the Gotham Writers Workshops. He lives in Anaheim, but to sound cooler, he usually says he "lives five minutes from Disneyland." He and his wife, Diana, have a home that is a registered California landmark. His burps smell like roses.

If Scott had not written this About page and someone else had, it would probably read like this: Scott Douglas lives in Anaheim with his wife. He is the author of other books. He likes to think that his organic deodorant holds back his BO for more than thirty minutes, but who is he kidding?